UNDERSTANDING

THE SPIRITUAL WORLD

A Ten Week Journey

WILLIAM M. WATSON, SJ

Other Books by William M. Watson SJ

Sacred Story:
An Ignatian Examen for the Third Millennium

FORTY WEEKS:
An Ignatian Path to Christ with Sacred Story Prayer

Inviting God into Your Life:
A Practical Guide for Prayer

Reflections and Homilies:
The Gonzaga Collection

Sacred Story Rosary:
An Ignatian Way to Pray the Mysteries

Sacred Story Affirmations

The Whole-Life Confession

My Sacred Story Missal

Sacred Story Press
1401 E Jefferson St, STE 405
Seattle, WA 98122

IMPRIMI POTEST
Rev. Scott R. Santarosa, S.J.

IMPRIMATUR
Bishop George V. Murry, S.J.
Bishop of Youngstown

ISBN-13:978-1539535010
ISBN-10:1539535010

Dedicated to Our Lady of the Way

Unless otherwise indicated, Scripture quotations are from the Holy Bible, *New American Bible, revised edition* © 2010, 1991, 1986, 1970 Confraternity of Christian Doctrine, Washington, D.C. The artwork for Night Vigils is in the public domain.

Jacket and Book Design: William Watson, SJ
Cover Photos: William Watson, SJ - St. Ignatius Chapel at Seattle University
Manufactured in the United States of America

CONTENTS

GRATITUDE

The author wishes to express his gratitude for guidance he has received

over the years from Jesuit spiritual directors; Gordon Moreland, Cliff

Jones, Jim Wise, Howard Gray, Joe McCormack, Michael Buckley, Jerry

Campbell, and former Jesuit now Trappist, Casey Bailey.

You have each guided me along the everlasting way.

For that I am a better man and priest.

Thank You.

FOREWORD

My introduction to the spiritual world began with an "inspiration" when I was eighteen years old. I saw a commercial for the Peace Corps while watching television late at night. The picture of poor people in Africa stirred in me a tremendous desire to give a year of my life to help them. As the night wore on, the inspiration took on intensity and depth. I decided that rather than serving for a year, I wanted to dedicate my life as a missionary. Nothing like this experience had ever happened to me before.

I never got to sleep that night I was so energized and hopeful. My best attempts to describe it are that it was like falling in love and knowing in an instant precisely what I wanted to do with my life. Although Catholic and a regular Mass attendee, I would not say that I had a real relationship with God or Christ.

Yet that night I experienced a spiritual force outside of myself that left me in awe and I remember saying to myself: "God is the source of this inspiration." I was overcome with joy. That was forty three years ago in the spring of 1973. It was my invitation from God to awaken spiritually so He could guide my life along the everlasting way.

In the forty-three years since my introduction to the spiritual world I can say that I am still in awe of the power of God and amazed at how much I still have to learn. So I write to you, dear friend, not as a master of the spiritual life but as one still on the journey. But if you have not yet embarked on the same journey or have for whatever reason stalled in your progress, I would like to extend you an invitation dive in.

This ten-week journey is a simplified and restructured introduction to spiritual discernment for my previous book: *Forty Weeks, An Ignatian Path to Christ with Sacred Story Prayer*. Many have asked for more resources on spiritual discernment and so we decided to do a new volume dedicated solely to this very important topic.

The goal of the present book is to help you attune the radar of your mind and heart to the spiritual world. You will discover three sources inspiring you: your own unique human nature; God, the creator of human nature; and the force St. Ignatius of Loyola calls "the enemy of human nature."

All three sources of inspiration consciously and/or unconsciously motivate everything you do in your life. Like breathing, you might not be aware you are being inspired, but you are. And like your breathing, God and your enemy are actively inspiring you 24/7 because both want you for eternity—God for eternal life—the enemy of human nature for eternal death. It is a cornerstone of our faith that the God of Light and the lord of darkness are real. That is why we need a roadmap for understanding how the forces of light and darkness work in the context of our own personal history.

God's passion to always help you should inspire hope and consolation. But the relentlessness of the enemy to derail your life should not frighten you. Those whose lives are committed to Christ should trust in him who overcame all darkness. And awakening to the spiritual world will be your key to more consciously cooperating with the inspirations of God and rejecting the inspirations of your enemy.

To help you do this I am inviting you to engage various spiritual exercises in the course of your days. The exercises will have times of quiet, times of prayer, times of physical exercise, times for reflection and journaling, times to turn off technology and open your heart and times to meditate in the evening hours on the Gospel stories of Jesus.

There will be short exercises upon waking and before you go to bed and you will also practice the Ignatian Examen prayer, meditating daily for fifteen minutes on the themes of Creation, Presence, Memory, Mercy and Eternity. If you are even moderately faithful to the exercises over these ten weeks, what you discover about the spiritual world will enlighten and amaze you.

Enjoy the spiritual exercises. Enjoy the journey. Throw the net of your heart out into deep water of the spiritual world. Your life will never be the same.

Fr. Bill Watson, S.J.
Feast of Christ the King

Beloved, do not trust every spirit but test the spirits
to see whether they belong to God, because
many false prophets have gone out into the world.
1 Jn 4: 1

Finally, draw your strength from the Lord and from his mighty
power. Put on the armor of God so that you may be able to stand
firm against the tactics of the devil. For our struggle is not with
flesh and blood but with the principalities, with the powers, with
the world rulers of this present darkness,
with the evil spirits in the heavens.
Therefore, put on the armor of God, that you may be able to resist
on the evil day and, having done everything, to hold your ground.
So stand fast with your loins girded in truth, clothed with
righteousness as a breastplate, and your feet
shod in readiness for the gospel of peace.
In all circumstances, hold faith as a shield, to quench all [the]
flaming arrows of the evil one. And take the helmet of salvation
and the sword of the Spirit, which is the word of God.
Eph 6: 12-17

INTRODUCTION

Entering the Spiritual World

Due to Original Sin, we have lost our capacity to readily distinguish truth from falsehood. To enter the path of discernment, to enter the spiritual world, we need to understand God and the universe God created. It is a universe that is both physical and spiritual. To help you attune your spiritual radar and enter the school of discernment, let me propose a relational model (or paradigm) for God, human persons, and the created universe. Let us take a few moments to explore this relational paradigm.[1]

First, we affirm God is Three Persons but One. We also affirm that God is Love. If God is Three Persons but One God and God is Love, we can affirm that God is Relationship made perfect by Love. God is a Trinity of perfect, loving relationships. The Trinity—Father, Son and Spirit—are three totally distinct, unique persons with no boundaries to their giving and receiving love. God is Love. God is One.

In classic Trinitarian theology, the reciprocal love of the Father and the

Son for each other is the Holy Spirit. The "three in one and one in three" however is not a scientific formula but a Love without beginning or end. God is Perfect Relationship.

Love is always about relationship. The loss of love is always about the breaking of relationship. So everything not of God is anti-relationship, what Scripture calls the spirit of anti-Christ, "which is to come, but is already in the world" (1 Jn 4: 3).

Second, we affirm that God "created mankind in his image; in the image of God He created them; male and female he created them" (Gen. 1:27). God *willed* human nature's form, freely creating persons as a perfect relationship of body and spirit.[2] The *human nature* God willed is the person as an *embodied spirit.* Human nature as *embodied spirit* is fashioned in God's own image. Consequently, persons are made to share in our own way in the Love that the Trinity enjoys. We are unique beings created to freely *give* and *receive* love with no boundaries.

Perfectly transparent in the *giving* and *receiving* of love: perfectly giving; perfectly accepted; perfectly loved; perfectly loving; and eternally cherished. This *giving and receiving* of love, with no boundaries, was intended in God's plan to be realized between the persons and their Creator, and between the persons themselves. The Trinity's free gift of the creation has as its apex the creation of persons crafted in the Divine image.

Third, the story of Paradise in the Book of Genesis reveals the state of *perfect relationship* between our first parents and God. This state of intimacy with God enabled a state of perfect justice and righteousness—a paradise! As long as our first parents remained in this state of spiritual intimacy with the Divine—as long as the state of perfect justice held—they were free from sickness and death.[3] This state of immortality was possible as long as they allowed God to be the very center of their lives—as long as they stayed in perfect, intimate relationship with God. In this state of perfect intimacy—their hearts undivided—they *knew themselves.* They had perfect interior harmony between their body and spirit.

Because they were innocent and radically transparent to their Creator, they cherished each *through God's eyes* as sacred. As incarnate spirits they shared intimate knowledge, respect, trust, complementarity, uniqueness, separateness and transcendent love. And they understood the creation because they were intimate with the Creator. They had perfect relationship with creation because they understood it as God's gift. God gifts the human persons with the *power to name* the plants and animals. We can understand that this gift of naming includes the knowledge of creation's rhythms. They would understand *how* creation works to their benefit and their delight and for their enjoyment. The gift of love freely given to our first parents by God was to expand in cosmic harmony.

Covering Their Nakedness

In Genesis 3: 7, Adam and Eve "see" their nakedness and "cover" themselves. Their *seeing* and *covering* demonstrates that their separation from God awakens them to know and feel that they no longer have control over their physical nature. They can objectify each other—use each other—and in their loss of innocence, are shamed by this discovery. Now begins the history of psychological and physical exploitation linked to the very gift God created to give life: human sexuality. The enemy of human nature knew this tragedy would result and relishes the agony it causes. The perfect complementarity of human nature created in the Divine image, male and female, is shattered by narcissism. But God has a plan to rescue us and make all things new. It begins with the miracle of the wine at the Wedding at Cana that signifies the super abundance of grace that God pours out upon the covenant of marriage through Christ's life. (Jn 2: 1-12).

Free will, essential for love, also allows persons to sever their relationship with Love, with God. The tragedy of Original Sin severs the perfect relationship between the incarnate spirits made in the Divine image and the Creator:

When they heard the sound of the Lord God walking about in the garden at the breezy time of the day, the man and his wife hid themselves from the Lord God among the trees of the garden. (Gen 3:8)

Relationship violated and severed is the *true face of sin*. The perfect relationship they had enjoyed now becomes filled with blame and grief. They will fight each other and their offspring will fight them. Their perfect relationship with creation is now also cursed (Gen 3:17-19) and they lose immortality. They are vulnerable to sickness and disease that God never intended (Ps 1: 13-15).

For God formed us to be imperishable; the image of his own nature he made us. But by the envy of the devil, death entered the world, and they who are allied with him experience it. (Wis 2:23-4).

With death and broken relationships on all sides, abandonment and loneliness are the heart's deepest fears. As the most profound misery caused by sin, it is what Christ suffered on the cross, for all of humanity for all time, to a degree unimaginable: *My God, my God, why have you abandoned m*e? Love itself, suffered love's complete absence (Ps 22: 1; Mt 27: 45-46).

But God's work in creation cannot be undone by sin. The *original* unity is lost forever, but out of this tragedy God creates an even more astonishing good. God would not create such beauty without a way to rectify the tragedy of Original Sin with something more glorious.[4]

We understand the glorious plan in the joyful Easter proclamation: "O happy fault, O necessary sin of Adam which gained for us so great a Redeemer!" "Instead of restoring man to what he had been, God has bent down from His eternity, taking him into His arms and pressing him to His heart in an embrace so close that the gulf between Creator and creature has been bridged, God and man henceforth forming in the order of grace a single being, 'the whole Christ.'"[5]

Human nature, broken and lost, is now united with the second person of the Trinity and made friends once again through Christ Jesus with God. We are now invited to accept the mission of participating with Christ in His grand work of Reconciliation. We do this by opening to life as *Sacred Story*. We allow God to work His miracle of healing and forgiveness for the hope that we, as brothers and sisters of Christ and children of God, are destined to share:

Human Nature and Authentic Identity

Films, songs, books and newspapers often define *human nature* positively *and solely* as our lower appetites. How these lower appetites might be divided from our spiritual nature and from Divine influence is usually ignored. Today, many definitions of human nature are influenced by the theories of Sigmund Freud. Freud believed that sexual drives/desires are the root of all human psychological activity. *Being authentic* often means discerning one's identity mainly by expressing one's sensual appetites. Yet to discern one's *authentic identity* requires being spiritually grafted to Christ. Only then can one discern both the higher calling we have as daughters and sons of God, and our true human nature. This "being born from above" reveals the truth about God, our authentic identity and our mission to love as Christ loved.

I consider that the sufferings of this present time are as nothing compared with the glory to be revealed for us. For creation awaits with eager expectation the revelation of the children of God; for creation was made subject to futility, not of its own accord but because of the one who subjected it, in hope that creation itself would be set free from slavery to corruption and share in the glorious freedom of the children of God. We know that all creation is groaning in labor pains even until now; and not only that, but we ourselves, who have the first fruits of the

Spirit, we also groan within ourselves as we wait for adoption, the redemption of our bodies. For in hope we were saved. Now hope that sees for itself is not hope. For who hopes for what one sees? But if we hope for what we do not see, we wait with endurance. In the same way, the Spirit too comes to the aid of our weakness; for we do not know how the Spirit too comes to the aid of our weakness; for we do not know how to pray as we ought, but the Spirit itself intercedes with inexpressible groanings. And the one who searches hearts knows what is the intention of the Spirit, because it intercedes for the holy ones according to God's will. (Rm 8: 18-27)

Your discernment and journey in the spiritual world is made easier if you can see everything in light of the *paradigm of perfect relationship*—given, lost, and being restored in Christ:

1) Perfect relationship of incarnate spirits in our unity of body and spirit.

2) Perfect relationship of created, incarnate spirits with our Creator God.

3) Perfect relationship of incarnate spirits with each other as unique individuals.

4) Perfect relationship between incarnate spirits as male and female called to fruitful, respectful, loving and joyful reverence.

5) Perfect relationship between created, incarnate spirits with the earth given for our delight, refreshment and sustenance.

6) Perfect relationship with the Church, the *Body of Christ*, as the community formed by Him for the work of Reconciliation, leading to a new heavens and a new earth.

Every thought, word and deed that seeks to *affirm the meaning* of perfect relationship and the human nature *willed* by God, everything that is working to heal damaged relationships, is a work of the Divine-Inspirer; God the Creator.

Every thought, word and deed that moves to *alter the meaning* of perfect relationship and the human nature *willed* by God, everything that is further undermining damaged relationships, is a work of the counter-inspirer; "the enemy of human nature," *who from the beginning, is a murderer and a liar—the father of lies* (Jn 8: 43-45).[6]

As you enter the journey into the spiritual world, keep your heart and mind focused on the *relational paradigm*. You are seeking the knowledge of your identity as a child of God, but informed by the truth of perfect relationship. Your authentic identity is a human nature, *willed* by God, as *unity* of body and spirit. You seek also the knowledge of your authentic God-given human nature as it has been violated and broken by Original Sin. And you seek this knowledge in light of what Christ is offering: by His life, death and resurrection, you are offered *the beginning* of the full healing that will be completed in the world and the life to come.

What is Truth?

"For this I was born and for this I came into the world, to testify to the truth. Everyone who belongs to the truth listens to my voice."
Pilate said to him, "What is truth?"
Jn 18: 37-8

At the beginning of the Third Millennium, many believe truth is relative. Even before the Third Millennium commenced, many pointed out that the greatest threat to the Faith is not atheism but relativism. Jesus tells Pilate that he was born and came into the world to testify to the truth—the truth about God, the truth about human nature, and the truth about salvation. Truth does exist and discernment's goal is to help us distinguish truth from falsehood in our *Sacred Story*.

In short, you are seeking the knowledge of perfect relationship and how in your own life and the world, that perfection has been broken but can also be restored, healed and redeemed by the Divine Physician. You are also seeking knowledge of the thief and the robber—*the enemy of human nature*—who seeks to distort what authentic relationship is, and to hide from you the Truth of God and your authentic human nature.

You are seeking to discern the two plot-lines in your story: the one that leads to curse and death and the one that leads to life and blessings. Ultimately, you are seeking to know truth from falsehood in *all* of your thoughts, words and deeds.

So Jesus said again, "Amen, amen, I say to you, I am the gate for the sheep. All who came [before me] are thieves and robbers, but the sheep did not listen to them. I am the gate.
Whoever enters through me will be saved, and will come in and go out and find pasture. A thief comes only to steal and slaughter and destroy; I came so that they might have life and have it more abundantly. I am the good shepherd.
A good shepherd lays down his life for the sheep.
(Jn 10: 7-11)

SPIRITUAL EXERCISES
FOR THE DAILY JOURNEY

On your ten-week journey in the spiritual world, you will be involved in daily exercises that will help you to build your discernment ability and tune your spiritual radar. The exercises are designed to help you grow closer to Christ by understanding and following his inspirations and to avoid the traps of the enemy of human nature by understanding and resisting his inspirations.

These rituals described below comprise a spiritual awakening method and are key elements of St. Ignatius' *Spiritual Exercises* and his *Examen* that have proven effective for hundreds of years. They are simple and practical and they work. I am also proposing times during the day to give yourself a break from technology so that you can more readily listen to the spiritual world.

I propose you practice these exercises as suggested—some every day, and others once a week. This page is your reference for the exercises for your excursion into the spiritual world. Don't beat yourself up if you can't do all of them every day. Do what you can and just keep moving forward!

1. When I Awake in the Morning—1 Minute Total

When you awaken, keep your eyes closed and "feel" the day before you. Are you anxious or hopeful?

Ask Christ to help you overcome the specific anxieties you experience.

Thank Him for the hopes you identify.
Before opening your eyes, offer your day to God with a Morning Prayer[7] and end by praying for protection to St. Michael the Archangel, Christ's lead guardian in the battle against evil.[8]

2. Morning Time—Twenty Minutes Total

For the first twenty minutes after getting up in the morning (including the 1 minute of "when I awake" prayer), keep free of all media and technology so that your heart has the necessary quiet time to access the spiritual world and your own heart.

3. Core Exercise Time—Fifteen Minutes Total

Take fifteen minutes to do the Ignatian *Examen* exercise discipline reflecting on Creation, Presence, Memory, Mercy and Eternity. Do it mid-day, mid-afternoon or just after the evening meal. We have extensive research to show that these times for praying this discipline are the best ones for keeping to the daily ritual and remaining faithful in its practice. You may want to download and use the MP3 version of the Ignatian Examen on our Sacred Story website.[9]

Find a quiet place apart, a place where you will not be disturbed by family, friends, or the things of the world. Bring with you any specific annoyances or strong emotional events you experienced today. Bring also your particular graces and inspirations.

During this time, kneel or sit, whichever is better suited to your prayer style and more conducive to contemplative reflection, prayer, and devotion.

Keep your eyes closed, or if opened, in a fixed position, not allowing them to roam.

Take 15-minutes for this exercise, *no more and no less*.

Consciously enter *the spiritual world* for these 15-minute periods in one of two ways both of which are proposed by St. Ignatius (try both and determine which best suits your character and personality).

First Way: Say the word "Creation" and continue meditating on this word as long as you find meaning, connections, delight, and inspirations—the positive graces you seek. The same method of reflection should be followed for each of the other words and for the meditations associated with each word (Presence, Memory, Mercy and

Eternity). You'll find those meditations below.

Second Way: With each breath or respiration, say "Creation" internally then from one breath to another say the word while you ponder the graces and inspirations you seek. During this same time, direct your attention mainly to the meaning of the word and graces you seek, the Person who is addressed, and why you need those graces. Follow this method with the other words (Presence, Memory, Mercy, Eternity) until you finish all the other meditations in the Examen prayer.

If my description of these two ways sounded a bit abstract, don't worry, everything will clarify as you move through the days and weeks. And no matter which way you choose, briefly at the beginning and at the end of the prayer time, *see* in your mind your whole life in God's hands. While breathing slowly and deeply, say inwardly the litany of: Creation, Presence, Memory, Mercy, and Eternity. Ignatius discovered that one of the best ways open your heart to God is through daily pondering these eternal truths.

Remember, for the body of the 15-minute prayer, after the opening litany, and before the closing litany, you can be flexible. On some days, you may spend equal amounts of time on each meditation. On other days, you may spend most of your time on one meditation. Let your heart lead you, based on the events of the day, and the images and emotions that emerge in your reflections. When praying, all roads lead to God.

EXAMEN PRAYER MEDITATIONS

As you move through your life remember, too, that this fifteen minute ritual can move with you—long after you have ended the Understanding the Spiritual World program. You can pray the whole 15-minute Sacred Story *prayer once or twice daily and consciously repeat to Christ Jesus the five-word refrain (Creation, Presence, Memory, Mercy, Eternity) whenever you are in the grip of fear, anxiety, sins, addictions, or destructive compulsions.*

CREATION
I believe God created everything in love and for love; I ask for heart-felt knowledge of God's love for me, and for gratitude for the general and particular graces of this day.

PRESENCE
I believe God is present in each moment and event of my life, and I ask for the grace to awaken, see and feel where and how, especially in this present moment.

MEMORY
I believe every violation of love committed by me and against me is in my memory, and I ask God to reveal them to me, especially those that have manifested themselves today, so I can be healed.

MERCY
I believe that forgiveness is the only path to healing and illumination. I beg for the grace of forgiveness, and the grace to forgive the general and particular failures in my past and of this day.

ETERNITY
I believe the grace of forgiveness opens my heart, making my every thought, word and deed bear fruit that endures to eternity. I ask that everything in my life serve Christ's Great Work of Reconciliation.

As the days and weeks progress, you will learn each meditation by heart. If you prefer, you can use the 15 minute guided meditation version of this prayer on our sacredstory.net website. Go to the Members tab on the website and become a member. It is free. Then go to Forty Weeks "Audio and Video Resources." On that page you will find an MP3 download called "Meditation." This is the entire Examen prayer in a guided format with music that you can listen to and follow along with your mind and heart.

Close the 15-minute *Examen* exercise with one or other of these two prayers:

Our Father
Our Father, who art in heaven, hallowed be Thy name.
Thy Kingdom come, Thy will be done, on earth, as it is in heaven.
Give us this day our daily bread, and forgive us our trespasses,
as we forgive those who trespass against us. Lead us not into temptation, but deliver us from evil. Amen.

(This is the prayer favored by Ignatius for this discipline).

Prayer for Generosity

Lord, teach me to be generous.
Teach me to serve you as you deserve;
to give and not to count the cost,
to fight and not to heed the wounds,
to toil and not to seek for rest,
to labor and not to ask for reward,
save that of knowing that I do your will.

(This is the prayer of St. Ignatius)

4. Day Time—One Contiguous Hour Total

Have one hour in the day where you use no media or technology. The time should be a contiguous hour and not several non-sequential time segments added together equaling an hour. Use this time to do the reading/reflection spiritual exercises for each day or just to enjoy the quiet. If you can't do a full hour, then try 45 or 30 minutes.

5. Evening Time—One Contiguous Half Hour Total

Turn off all technology and media one half hour before going to bed. This will help you access the spiritual world and also sleep better. Use this time also to spend 1-2 minutes to do your Daily Spiritual Journal.

6. Daily Spiritual Journal—1-2 Minutes Once Daily

Once you begin the journey you will be aware of new spiritual movements in your life. Writing them in your *Exercise Record* will help you build the discipline to understand and work with your spiritual life. This book has an Exercise Record for each day of the journey so if you have your book, you have your Record. Keep it with you when you do your structured 15-minute exercise periods and at the end of the day. Write your journal entries in your own hand. Writing long-hand is a greater expression of your spirit than typing.

Write in your Record daily, after you end your last *Examen* 15-minute prayer session. What you write should be only single words or short phrases. The goal is to track the most significant events from your days.

CONSOLATIONS: On the graced end of the scale, you are looking for gratitude, hope, and peace and the daydreams and fantasies coming from the Divine-Inspirer. So look for those things that increase your faith, your hope and your love of God and your neighbor.

DESOLATIONS: Make sure to look for destructive patterns and trends in your life: patterns of fear, anger and grief, and patterns of sin, compulsion and addiction. In both of these patterns you are also looking for links to persons, events, or issues that decrease your faith, your hope and your love of God and neighbor.

The patterns and trends that St. Ignatius thought were most productive to focus on for spiritual growth and are most relevant to this journey are those that help you identify damaging, addictive, sinful habits *at their roots*. So remain aware of patterns and trends that reveal the *triggering mechanisms* that make you easy prey—these may be patterns and trends from you early life that have become 'sources' the 'origins' and 'roots' of bad habits. We might put it into a helpful phrase like this: "Where you fall, there dig for gold! Or: "Where you find difficulties will be the main source of your spiritual growth!"

Every day, take one minute before going to bed to write your brief Exercise Record entry. Remember your day's awakening exercises, and ask for the grace to be aware of the importance of any significant events that open you to anger, fear, grief or temptations, failures and sins. Ask for God's grace to see your life integrated and holistic as God does.

God *longs* to be with you and lead you to freedom, forgiveness, peace and healing. *As you read these instructions now you might say, "I don't know...this seems like a lot of work," but remember,* people like you who have engaged the Exercises gained much more from the entire journey method than those who did not write in their journal.

And those who persevered in the journal practice are the ones who learned to be brief and to write no more than a few words or a short phrase. I can promise you: y*ou will not succeed in the journal practice if you take more than a minute or two a day to accomplish it!* Be brief, but specific and address Jesus in your notes. Here is an example to help you focus:

1) **CONSOLATION**: Jesus, the letter I received today from my brother brought me peace because it made me realize God will help me every step of the way.

2) **DESOLATION**: Jesus, I felt like I would never overcome some of my bad habits today and I felt very discouraged. Help me not lose hope in you or myself.

8 As I Lay Down to Sleep—1 Minute Total

Pray for your loved ones by name.
Are you anxious or hopeful? Ask Christ to help
you overcome your specific anxieties.
Thank Christ for the hopes you identify.
Ask God to be present in your dreams.
End by asking your spiritual guardian to stand watch through the night.

9. Night Vigils—30 to 45 Minutes A Week

You are being invited to spend thirty to forty-five minutes in a guided Ignatian meditation on a Gospel story each week. Hopefully you have the option of doing this at a church that has a 24 hour adoration option, but you can also do it at home. You can choose to do this on Thursday, Friday, Saturday or Sunday.

These night vigils will appear at the end of day seven of each week. The Night Vigils can substitute for the Evening Time Exercise. If that is your choice, do nothing after these vigils but go home, do your journal, then go to bed.

The Night Vigils are best done between the hours of 10 PM to 1 AM when the night becomes quiet and you can more readily have access to the spiritual world. Depending on your schedule and level of energy, you may decide it best to do them earlier.

10. Reconciliation-Thirty Minutes a Month

This ten-week journey asks you to use the great sacrament of Reconciliation to focus your heart, experience the mercy of Jesus and clear away the junk in your life that blocks your ready access to grace.

Spiritual exercise is even more important than physical exercise. Many of the results of spiritual exercise will have a far greater impact on your whole life.

It is work, it is exercise, but you will be amazed at the world that opens up to you by engaging it with a diligent passion! A recent study by the Catholic Leadership Institute said that the frequency of the reception of Reconciliation is the biggest difference between:

✠   Those who have encountered Jesus and are growing as disciples and
✠   Those who say Jesus Christ is the most important relationship in their life.

This practice opens your heart to forgiveness and peace and makes you a more committed disciple of the Lord Jesus. Take advantage of its powerful graces on your spiritual journey of life.

11. Journal at Week's End—5 Minutes Total

On Sunday (or Saturday if that is your "week's end"), in place of the day's end journal exercise, review the consolation and desolation phrases from the preceding week.

Notice what particular insights or inspirations arise as you review the short phrases. Then write one sentence for the pattern of consolation and desolation that seems to you to be the most significant of the week.

Write these insights on the two NOTES pages after the Day Seven exercises. Date these reflections so you can watch your growth as the Exercises progress.

12. Journal at Month's End—5 Minutes Total

At the end of a month, in place of the week's end journal exercise, review your summary insights from these end-of-week exercises. Look for any patterns that are emerging. As you see patterns, write short comments ("I think..." "I believe..." "I discovered...") that reveal any changes you experience in your life as a result of grace, healing, forgiveness, or the insights you receive. Write these also on the NOTES pages after Day Seven.

Example: "I've figured out now that not making the "a" group and feeling that loss of confidence is linked to the very same issue that made me hope my brother would always be there to help me. Earlier in my life it was my brother who built up my confidence and now he's not around so I need to focus on the hope he gave me and now give it to myself through Christ. This will help me to not let myself get discouraged by false messages in my everyday life that tell me: 'I am no good'."

Spiritual World Daily Exercise Record

In every chapter of this ten-week journey, for every day of every week, you are invited to keep a record of your daily spiritual exercises. There is a record for each day of each week of Understanding the Spiritual World.

One goal in filling this out is to see the exercises you complete and don't complete. The ideal would be, of course, to complete all the exercises every day, but that will not always be possible. By having the record you can see patterns that might help you become more faithful or gain insights as to why you are not faithful.

For example, if you notice that you generally don't complete your daily exercises because you just can't turn your smartphone off for a half hour, you can work with that, pray about it, ask for help to change that pattern.

If you do other exercises but miss the journal exercise regularly, perhaps you'll see a pattern related to when you go to sleep—maybe you are not going to sleep early enough, and your whole schedule is off-kilter. You can fix that.

Having the exercise record will help you not only to more fruitfully engage the ten-week journey, but also to improve your life. Fill-in the locations for the next day's exercises before you go to bed. This will really help you focus your attention on the journey and enable you to be more faithful to the daily disciplines.

EXERCISE RECORD

1. When I Awake in the Morning—1 Minute Minimum - 2 Maximum

Location_____ I Exercised Yes____(____Minutes) No____

2. Morning Time Exercise—10 Minutes Minimum -20 Minutes Maximum

Location_____ I Exercised Yes____(____Minutes) No____

3. Examen Exercise Time—15 Minutes Maximum

Location_____ I Exercised Yes____(____Minutes) No____

4. Day Time Exercise—60 Contiguous Minutes (30 or 45 if 60 is not possible)

Location_____ I Exercised Yes____(____Minutes) No____

5. Evening Time Exercise—30 Contiguous Minutes Minimum – 60 Maximum

Location_____ I Exercised Yes____(____Minutes) No____

6. Exercise Journal—1-2 Minutes Once Daily

Location_____ I Exercised Yes____(____Minutes) No____

7. As I Lay Down to Sleep—1 Minute Total

Location_____ I Exercised Yes____(____Minutes) No____

8. Night Vigils—30 minutes minimum – 45 maximum

Location_____ I Exercised Yes____(____Minutes) No____

Desolation From the Day – <u>Write no more than two sentences</u> on what decreased your faith, your hope and your love for God and neighbor today.

Consolation From the Day – <u>Write no more than two sentences</u> on what increased your faith, your hope and your love for God and neighbor today.

<u>There are two blank pages at the end of each week for your daily and weekly notes and reflections</u>

Finding the Name for God or Jesus
That Speaks to Your Heart

Before embarking on your spiritual journey, it will be most beneficial to uncover the name for God, Jesus or the Spirit that speaks most directly to your heart. One of the things you want to do on this journey (and for all of your life) is to talk directly to God from your heart. Pray to be inspired on which name touches you most deeply.

For this exercise, go to a church and sit in the presence of the Blessed Sacrament or go to your place of prayer in your home. Once you are settled in your place of prayer, ask for God's inspiration to uncover the name for God that speaks most directly to your heart. Then ask, in words from your heart, to be inspired to discover or remember the most intimate and/or meaningful name for God the Father, Son and Spirit that you have used in prayer.

The name will resonate deeply in your heart and reflect God's relationship to you and your personal relationship with God. The following may be helpful:

Merciful Father, Loving Father, Almighty Father, Our Father, Father God, Loving Creator, Creator God, God of Love, My God, Holy God, Father of the Poor, God of All Mercy, God of All Compassion, Father of Jesus, Lord Jesus Christ, Lord Jesus, Christ Jesus, Dear Jesus, Adorable Jesus, Adorable Christ, Good Jesus, Jesus, Merciful Savior, Jesus My Savior, Son of God, Dearest Lord, My Lord, My Lord and My God, Sacred Heart of Jesus, Lamb of God, Good Shepherd, Crucified Savior, Holy Spirit, Spirit of Jesus, Spirit of the Lord, Loving Spirit, Holy Spirit of God, Love of God, Divine Spirit, Creator Spirit, Creator God.

Ask for the grace to discover the name for God that touches your heart most intimately. You will know the right name because it has the power to unlock your trust and your love, and to stir your affections.

Write the name for God or Jesus in your notebook when you discover it. From this point forward, use this name when you address God or Jesus Christ. The Trinity delights when you to speak directly from your heart.[10]

SAINT IGNATIUS' STORY

St. Ignatius is the inspiration for this ten-week journey so taking some time to reflect on his life and conversion will be worth your while. His story is in three parts. You can do it on one sitting on a single day. Or you can spread it out over three days and take your time to let the story sink in and have an impact on your heart and mind. You will know best how much time to take.

Part One: St. Ignatius and His Legacy

A Fallen Soldier

Until his thirtieth year Ignatius Loyola was unconscious of the sacredness of his life. Instead, he was sincerely devoted to life's pleasures and vanities. His life was not easy. Ignatius' mother died when he was an infant and his father died when he was sixteen. Perhaps that had some impact on his personality. He was a gambling addict, sexually self-indulgent, arrogant, hotheaded and insecure.

By our contemporary measures, Ignatius' family was dysfunctional. Was this person a possible candidate for sainthood? It did not look promising. But God does not judge by human standards. It is God's nature to pursue all who have fallen asleep through sin, addiction and selfishness. God judges the heart; with unbounded grace and patient mercy God reaches into the ruins that sin makes of our lives and transforms them into *Sacred Stories*.

Ignatius, with all his narcissism, psychological problems and sinful vices, was awakened by God's great love. A failed military campaign and a shattered leg forced him into a lengthy convalescence. Ignatius' time of recuperation provided an opportunity for Love to shine a light on much more serious and life-threatening wounds that were spiritual, emotional and psychological in nature.

These wounds were supported by the evolution of a destructive, sinful narcissism. For thirty years Ignatius' narcissism had rendered him unconscious to his true human nature and oblivious to his life as *Sacred Story*. The pleasures he indulged in and the power he wielded functioned like a narcotic to numb the pain of his hidden spiritual and psychological wounds. His sinful vices and self-indulgent pleasures blinded him to his authentic human nature and a fruitful life guided by a well-formed conscience.

God's grace reached into the reality of Ignatius' life and awakened in him a desire for innocence. His long-buried aspirations for living authentically suddenly became his prime motivation. He noticed it first while convalescing at Loyola. He became aware of new desires and a different energy while he daydreamed in reading stories of Christ and the saints. Pondering the saints' lives he imagined himself living a different, selfless life.

He compared these new daydreams to his usual vain, narcissistic daydreams. The old daydreams drew energy from a life of sin, addiction and vice while the daydreams of selfless generosity produced their own energy. Ignatius noticed a significant difference between the two sets of daydreams and the feelings they produced. The vain fantasies entertained him when he was thinking about them. But he noticed that when he set them aside, he felt empty and unsatisfied.

The new holy daydreams also entertained him when he was thinking about them. Yet when he set these aside, he remained content and felt an enduring calm and quiet joy. By paying close attention to the ultimate affective signatures of these two sets of daydreams and discerning their difference, Ignatius made a discovery that transformed his life and the history of Christian spirituality.

The Voice of Conscience

Ignatius discovered that the new, selfless aspirations were influenced by Divine inspirations. He further discovered that these inspirations reflected his true human nature and that the vain fantasies deadened his conscience. His narcissistic daydreams led him away from enduring peace because they masked his authentic human nature.

The old daydreams were powerful, ego affirming, and familiar. He knew in his heart that living their fantasy was the path to self-destruction. On the one hand he would be judged successful by the standards of the world, a world that measured success in terms of riches, honors, and pride. On the other hand, he would be judged a failure by the standards of the Gospel, standards that advocated a life of spiritual poverty, humility and consequential service—a *Sacred Story* that endures to eternal life.

Ignatius was awakened to the emotional wisdom and spiritual truth of his new daydreams. He became aware of the significant damage that his old lifestyle had done to both himself and others. What had been awakened in him was the divine gift of conscience, and with it, Ignatius experienced profound regret and sorrow for having wasted so much of his life on self-indulgent pleasures and fantasies, seductions that could never bring him lasting peace and satisfaction. He began to understand that living in pleasure and fantasy destroyed his authentic human nature and silenced his deepest desires.

As usually happens when people respond to the grace of conversion, Ignatius' new aspirations confused and disconcerted many of his closest family members and friends. Nonetheless he acted on these aspirations. Ignatius was now able to understand a path to God, a *pattern of conversion* that countless thousands would imitate.

A Menacing Fear Unmasked

After some months of living in the light of these new positive virtues, habits, and Divine inspirations, Ignatius was suddenly gripped by terror and panic. How could he manage to live the rest of his life without the pleasures of the past? It was easy to live virtuously for some months, but for the rest of his life? This was a real crisis because Ignatius began to wonder if this was an impossible goal.

Ignatius had two vital insights about this menacing fear. First, he realized it was a counter-inspiration prompted by the *enemy of his true human nature*. The panicky fear led him to think that it would be impossible to live virtuously for such a long time. Second, the counter-inspiration tempted him to return to his old narcissistic vices and habits. Seduced by their powerful influence, Ignatius would abandon all hope for a life of virtue. In essence, Ignatius was tempted to surrender living the authentic life that had finally brought him peace. He sensed an evil source inspiring this menacing fear and he challenged it head-on: "You pitiful thing! Can you even promise me one hour of life?"

A Decisive and Enduring Commitment to Remain Awake

Ignatius dismissed the counter-inspiration and its evil author by re-committing to this new wakefulness for the remainder of his life. This was Ignatius' second insight: NEVER trust the messages prompted by menacing fears. Counter them with a firm commitment to stay the course, to awaken and remain conscious.

This decisive, enduring commitment to persevere restored tranquility, and his fear abated. Ignatius had discovered, unmasked and confronted the deceiver. In this Ignatius learned another lesson about speaking truth to power that would guide his new life and help shape his first set of foundational discernment principles.

Ignatius had to face these same fears many, many more times. Eventually he knew they were false fears, *inspirations* of the enemy of his human nature. Most importantly, he gradually learned how to diffuse them, and to defend against them.

Our Christian life is a labor of love. In order for God's love to heal us we must do our part to open ourselves to God's graces. This requires conscious and ongoing effort to abstain from sinful, addictive habits in thoughts, words and deeds. There is a need to pray for God's grace. First we must awaken to that grace. With that same grace, we have the strength to resist and abstain from sinful, addictive attitudes and behaviors, both spiritual and material. God's grace makes our spiritual disciplines fruitful, activating the on-going healing of our human nature. Grace helps us climb out of the spiritual, mental physical and emotional ruts of our bound self toward a future of increased hope, holiness and balance and freedom.

Part Two: A Journey to the Heart

Ignatius in Control

Ignatius' decisive and enduring commitment to his conversion launched him directly into the center of his heart's brokenness and the pride masking those wounds. After leaving home Ignatius traveled to Montserrat and spent three days reviewing his life. It was at this time that he made a general confession of all his past sins. This first life confession initiated an enduring habit of weekly confession and communion. In this written confession Ignatius consciously detailed his sinful attitudes, behaviors and passions: gambling addiction, sexual self-indulgence, arrogance, and violent outbursts of temper. It took three days to write the story of his past life.

Yet he discovered that simply detailing and confessing his sinful habits and addictions did not disarm them. That would require going deeper to their source in his heart and history. Only in these deepest recesses could he confront the pattern of spiritual and psychological dysfunction that was most responsible for eroding his freedom and distorting his authentic human nature.

It is this inward journey that fully awakened his conscience. It was only at this depth that he discovered his authentic human nature and regained the creativity of childlike innocence. We do well to understand the tipping point of Ignatius' life from his root vices and narcissism to his new life of wakefulness, light, peace and hope. This is how his story unfolded.

Ignatius' new, pious habit of regular confession evolved into a destructive obsessive and compulsive torture. He confessed and re-confessed past sins multiple times, never feeling he had gotten to the bottom of his immoral deeds. This excruciating spiritual and psychological torment lasted for months. He was so anguished by his obsessive guilt that numerous times he wanted to commit suicide by throwing himself off the cliff where he prayed.

Even awareness of the emotional damage caused by this obsessive confession habit did not help him surrender it. Instead he initiated new, harsher physical disciplines and spiritual regimens. His goal was to gain complete control and self-mastery over his immoral and dissolute past. He wanted to remember every detail of his past sins so he could be perfectly cleansed, but nothing worked.

Finally, exhausted and disgusted with his efforts, he realized he intensely despised the spiritual life he was living. Ignatius had an urgent and compelling desire to "stop it!" This thought alarmed Ignatius, and his spiritual radar went on high alert. Ignatius discerned the inspiration came from another source but what could it be? He discovered the inspiration's origin and author only by understanding where the inspiration was taking him. It occurred to him that the inspiration was leading him in the same direction as the menacing fear he had previously experienced. Inspired to abandon his newly awakened life, Ignatius was being tempted to abandon the peace, the service to others, and the virtuous life of his *Sacred Story*. But *how* did this counter-inspiration succeed in gaining control? Ignatius realized it was rooted in his damaging confession habit and so he ceased the habit then and there of re-confessing past sins.

Surrendering Control to Embrace Powerlessness & Innocence

Ignatius' description in his *Autobiography* to stop his damaging confession habit appears inconsequential. But the choice was the most significant spiritual decision in his entire life. It was also the most difficult, because that one choice meant fully surrendering his life to God. It meant admitting his powerlessness over his sins and in humility allowing God, not himself, to be the source of his holiness.

Reflecting on the temptation to walk away from his new Christian life, Ignatius received an insight that the burdensome, destructive habit of re-confessing past sins was rooted in a pride to try and save himself. This pride forced him to his knees. On seeing this he "awoke as if from a dream," and was given the grace to stop the habit.

Ignatius' first life confession at Montserrat documented the *visible* manifestations of this deep distortion in his human nature. The Divine Physician next led Ignatius to the source of those visible sins. It was his wounded human nature that fueled the controlling, narcissistic personality. The pattern of *visible* sins, vices and addictions was only the tip of the iceberg.

From that moment of surrender at Manresa, Ignatius acknowledged his powerlessness and surrendered control of his life to God. For his entire life God waited to transform Ignatius' deepest desires into a *Sacred Story* whose legacy would endure to eternity. This *surrender* defines Ignatius' second set of foundation discernment principles.

An outpouring of mystical grace flooded Ignatius at this point. More importantly a humble and obedient spirit was beginning to emerge which enabled him to respond to the slightest movements of God's grace in his thoughts, words and deeds. In this humility and docility he discovered a life of service that changed the Church and the world. Later in life he reflected:

There are very few who realize what God would make of them if they abandoned themselves entirely to His hands, and let themselves be formed by His grace. A thick and shapeless tree trunk would never believe that it could become a statue, admired as a miracle of sculpture...and would never consent to submit itself to the chisel of the sculptor who, as St. Augustine says, sees by his genius what he can make of it. Many people who, we see, now scarcely live as Christians, do not understand that they could become saints, if they would let themselves be formed by the grace of God, if they did not ruin His plans by resisting the work which He wants to do.

The proud narcissist, the man who was master of his own universe, became a humble and obedient servant of the universe's true Master and Creator. To arrive at this point, Ignatius had to admit his powerlessness. He had to surrender control over his life and the distorted aspects of his human nature that had evolved over the years. He had to learn how to live out of his newly emerging authentic self, his *true* human nature previously hidden behind his wounded heart.

Ignatius also learned how to dismantle the narcissism that had evolved over the first thirty years of his life. The counter-inspirer, the enemy of his human nature, had cleverly concealed his true human nature and Ignatius had to begin life over again, this time allowing God to reveal his authentic self. This was why, after the resolution of this greatest of his life's crises, Ignatius experienced himself being taught by God. It was, he said, exactly like "a child is taught by a schoolmaster."

The Divine-Inspirer and the counter-inspirer

This harrowing crisis taught Ignatius a most vital lesson about counter-inspirations. The willpower and resolute commitment to live virtuously for the rest of his life could be manipulated and turned against him by means of subtle *inspirations*. What seemed like a holy, pious, and noble practice—a serious approach to confession—evolved into a damaging habit that made him loathe his spiritual life, and in frustration, *inspired* him to abandon it. He learned that the counter-inspirations of the enemy of his human nature could act like "an angel of light." These inspirations appear holy but when followed, they end in disaster, distancing one from God and from one's authentic self.

The counter-inspirer conceals our original wounds, counseling and guiding our steps to build a false identity, an anti-story, characteristically identified by a distorted ego and defended by narcissism. Our narcissistic pride rationalizes the habits, vices, addictions and lifestyles that form our anti-story. The counter-inspirer renders us unconscious to our *Sacred Story* and to our true Divinely shaped human nature.

God led Ignatius through this distorted evolution back to the lost innocence of his true human nature. The shattering of his powerful defenses and the unmasking of his prideful, narcissistic ego proved to be the tipping point of Ignatius' entire conversion process.

Wakefulness, Holiness and Heightened Consciousness

Ignatius' conversion from his anti-story and his full awakening to his *Sacred Story* was not a single event but rather a gradual process. His full evolution from a vain egomaniac to a saint took the rest of his life. His was a gradual, steady evolution from a sinful narcissist in control of his own life to an innocent, obedient servant of God. Growth in holiness requires desire, patience and daily effort to awaken to our authentic human nature. It takes time for grace to penetrate the influence of our anti-story so that our *Sacred Story* can more fully emerge. There are no short cuts to holiness, not even for saints.

A Life-Long Commitment to Christ in the Church

If you desire to surrender your anti-story and open to your *Sacred Story*, grace will awaken you, like Ignatius, to places in your heart's memories you might not wish to visit. The awakening will begin like Ignatius'. It starts with an honest identification of the *visible* manifestations of those spiritual and psychological distortions in the particulars of your human nature. These distortions disclose your lost innocence and a heart broken by the Original Fall and the cumulative sins of your family, clan and culture. Ignatius started this process with his life confession. He truthfully identified the habits, addictions, sins and compulsions characteristic of his lost innocence and broken heart.

Open yourself to the graces that will illumine the distinctive narcissistic elements fueling your sinful, compulsive behaviors. Ignatius needed much grace to overcome his defenses and unlock this hidden truth about his life. Everyone who embraces this path can confidently rely on the same grace to successfully navigate the journey to the center of one's heart. As confused as life is due to Original Sin, the Lord can and does penetrate our hearts and leads us to truth.

More tortuous than anything is the human heart, beyond remedy; who can understand it? I, the LORD, explore the mind and test the heart, Giving to all according to their ways, according to the fruit of their deeds (Jer 17: 9-10).

Part Three: The Call to Universal Reconciliation

Your Sacred Story

As with Ignatius, God extends an invitation to awaken to the pattern of spiritual, emotional and psychological dysfunction that has formed our anti-story. God invites us to awaken to our lives as *Sacred Story* and to produce fruit that endures to eternity. The awakening and growth will reveal where our freedom is compromised and how we close our hearts to our authentic human nature. Christ compassionately shows us how our selfishness and pride have corrupted our creativity, robbing us of the joy of innocence. God's invitation is gentle. God's awakening is merciful. Rest assured that God's passion is to pursue us, rescue us, heal us and bring us back to our original innocence. God's passion is Personal. God's passion is Love. God's passion is Christ Jesus. Be Not Afraid!

God's intention is to gradually heal and transform our thoughts, words and deeds. For every thought, word and deed influences my history in the direction of an anti-story or a *Sacred Story*. Every thought, word and deed, for good or ill, touches all people in my life, all the world and all of creation, shaping history's final chapter. The effects of sin and narcissism—as well as the effects of virtue and selflessness—have individual, social, physical, spiritual, and ecological ramifications that reach to the ends of creation. For everything and everyone is one in Love—one in Christ Jesus—through whom and for whom everything was made (Rom 11:36).

Every thought, word, or deed, no matter how discreet, has positive or negative significance in the interconnected web of life that God has fashioned through Christ. It is Christ's being—His SACRED STORY—that links each of our individual *Sacred Stories*. It is in Christ that the entire cosmos is joined together. God in Christ has made us responsible for and dependent upon each other and upon the earth that sustains us.

The Christ of the Cosmos—through whom and for whom everything was made—became man, and confronted, absorbed, and diffused all the destructive force of evil's evolutionary anti-history running through human nature and the created cosmos. Christ reconciles in Himself everything in the heavens and on the earth to bring peace to all by the blood of His cross. His SACRED STORY redeems and renews every chapter in our history, individual and collective.

Christ Jesus passionately awaits our participation to join His work of universal reconciliation. Our willingness to accept the path of conversion entails truthfully identifying our sins, dysfunction and addictions. It entails experiencing and admitting our powerlessness to save ourselves. It requires the patience of a lifetime while Christ writes our *Sacred Story*.

My participation in Christ's work of reconciliation is the only worthy vocation and the only labor that produces fruit enduring to eternity. My accepting the invitation unlocks the very mystery of life. When I accept the invitation, Christ promises to share His universal glory. Accepting the invitation to intentionally enter my *Sacred Story* has momentous consequences.

Now is the Time to Wake from Sleep

Our time on this earth is so very brief. Since the time of Christ's birth, life, death and resurrection, our story can only be measured and valued in light of His eternal mission of Reconciliation. Intentionally entering my *Sacred Story* will, over time, enable me to know God more intimately and serve God more generously. Like Ignatius, I am called to awaken from sleep—to awaken to wholeness and holiness. I was created and infused with the gift to awaken to a life that reverences the God, who in Christ and the Holy Spirit, is present in all things—all persons, and all creation.

Awakening to my *Sacred Story*, like Ignatius, calls for courage in the cleansing of the spirit and psyche that it initiates. The process requires discipline in the face of temptation and monotony. It requires consciously asking, even begging if necessary, for God's graces. It requires time and patience; deliberately choosing each day to be faithful to time and space for God. Awakening requires the patience of a lifetime. The journey is rich with blessings beyond our wildest expectations. Encountering Christ daily in *Sacred Story* forever changes life, relationships, the earth, and eternity.

What is needed for the journey will be provided each day. In my journey through the memories and experiences, past and present, I am promised the power and mercy of the LOVE that maintains and guides the entire cosmos. It is this LOVE that waits to transform your sins, addictions, angers, fears, grief, guilt and shame. It is this LOVE that restores your broken heart into a vessel of forgiveness, light and peace. The more embedded and impenetrable the web of darkness, compulsion, sin, and addiction in your life, the more strategic and magnificent is God's grace in breaking its grip, for nothing is impossible with God (Lk 1:37).

Your Sacred History

There are no short cuts to the story's unfolding. Conversion is lifelong but measurable when I intentionally, daily, consistently, and faithfully enter my *Sacred Story*. Recall that Christ Jesus Himself has traveled the path. He will guarantee my journey's safe passage and carry my burdens, failures, shame, broken heart, and confusion.

I will hold in my heart the humble example of Jesus washing my feet. He endured humiliations, torture, and a disgraceful death, so that I can find hope and healing for everything in my life that needs healing, forgiveness, and redemption. From the beginning of time His *SACRED STORY* is mystically imprinted into the souls of His chosen people and the Church. Through the pattern of His *STORY*, I, the Church, and all people can have their history rewritten as *Sacred Story*.

I will intentionally enter my life narrative for 15-minute intervals once or twice each day. My story linked to Christ's *SACRED STORY* and to all people and to all creation, runs from my birth in all the thoughts, words and deeds to shape my destiny here, and in the hereafter. The prayer will help me attune to Creation, Presence, Memory, Mercy, and

Eternity. When I encounter the fears, stresses, angers, temptations, failures, addictions and sins in my day, I can briefly attune to Creation, Presence, Memory, Mercy, and Eternity, and ask for the grace to see my whole story. By so doing, the Divine Physician can heal me and awaken my heart to its true human nature.

Christ extends the invitation and His Love, at the Heart of the Universe, awaits my response. I pray for the courage and generosity to enter with Christ into my *Sacred Story* on this ten-week journey. Be Not Afraid!

Week 1

Day One

Spiritual Exercise for Day or Evening

Mario Beauregard, Ph.D. is a neuroscience researcher whose specialty is human consciousness. In two books (*The Spiritual Brain* and *Brain Wars*) he documents how the old understanding of a purely material world must give way to a spiritual understanding of the human person and the cosmos. In multiple experiments, he showed that our power of consciousness can extend beyond our physical being to impact physical reality outside ourselves. In one instance, individuals were asked to "think" about turning on and off an electronic switch that was two rooms away. They were able to do this proving that consciousness is an energy that is not restricted to our physical body.

Understanding the Spiritual World is all about learning the art and discipline of spiritual discernment. I want to you think about this art/discipline in relation to your human consciousness as energy that reaches beyond you. The Catholic tradition would call that aspect of your human nature your "spiritual nature."

Saint Paul refers to this spiritual world and discernment with this language from the sixth chapter of his letter to the Ephesians: "For our struggle is not with flesh and blood but with the principalities, with the powers, with the world rulers of this present darkness, with the evil spirits in the heavens."

Because your consciousness is energy and your spiritual nature has a power to connect to any spiritual energy, good or evil, you need to develop your "radar" to understand the signals that are reaching you from the spirits in the heavens: some are holy and others are evil.

The challenge we face in developing that radar is complicated by the fact that holy energy can upset us and evil energy can excite us. We

---

Evil's Work is More Hidden than Sensational

Don't go looking for *Exorcist*-movie drama in your spiritual discernment. The counter-inspirer accomplished his greatest damage in the Original Sin when human nature was crippled. He knew you would be subject to disease and death, and that the anger, cynicism, sickness, war, poverty and injustice in human society would chip away at belief. The loss of faith, hope and love would result, and belief in a "God of love" would diminish. Kindness avoided, forgiveness withheld and self-centered behavior work to diminish faith, hope and love. All have conspired to create the evolution of darkness present in our history. *Exorcist*-movie evil does exist but serves the counter-inspirer's work mostly by making us blind to evil's greatest work: crushing the human spirit and making us believe that evil is more powerful than God and love. Yet, the enemy of human nature— the counter-inspirer—has already lost his battle in Christ's victory. Be Not Afraid!

---

need to learn the difference by the direction each energy force points. Do not worry. With your fidelity to the Exercises and the instructions you receive, you will become adept in this most ancient and important of disciplines. There is nothing more valuable for the Christian to learn that the discipline of "spiritual discernment."

For your Exercise today, I want you to say the phrases below as often as they come into your mind. Say them audibly and as you do realize that the "spiritual consciousness" of your unique human nature is an energy force as vast as the cosmos!

My life is a force of spiritual energy.

Spirits both holy and evil seek to guide me.

I will cooperate with the holy and reject the evil.

I will learn the difference between the two.

EXERCISE RECORD

1. When I Awake in the Morning—1 Minute Minimum - 2 Maximum

Location_____ I Exercised Yes___(___Minutes) No___

2. Morning Time Exercise—10 Minutes Minimum -20 Minutes Maximum

Location_____ I Exercised Yes___(___Minutes) No___

3. Examen Exercise Time—15 Minutes Maximum

Location_____ I Exercised Yes___(___Minutes) No___

4. Day Time Exercise—60 Contiguous Minutes (30 or 45 if 60 is not possible)

Location_____ I Exercised Yes___(___Minutes) No___

5. Evening Time Exercise—30 Contiguous Minutes Minimum – 60 Maximum

Location_____ I Exercised Yes___(___Minutes) No___

6. Exercise Journal—1-2 Minutes Once Daily

Location_____ I Exercised Yes___(___Minutes) No___

7. As I Lay Down to Sleep—1 Minute Total

Location_____ I Exercised Yes___(___Minutes) No___

Desolation From the Day – Write no more than two sentences on what decreased your faith, your hope and your love for God and neighbor today.

Consolation From the Day – Write no more than two sentences on what increased your faith, your hope and your love for God and neighbor today.

Week 1

Day Two

Spiritual Exercise for Day or Evening

I will go for a thirty minute walk or run or find a quiet place to sit where I can see nature. I will not listen to music or bring my cell phone with me. I will listen instead to my daydreams, nature, and the people I pass by. I will notice people who appear happy and those who seem to be struggling. I will listen to and watch the world God made for my enjoyment, appreciation and engagement. I realize that I have spiritual energy that reaches to the end of the cosmos and beyond. I will attune my radar to what is holy and reject what is evil. I will listen to what brings me joy or makes me sad.

At the end of your walk, run or quiet time speak to God from your heart and ask God to help you with the one thing you need most today in developing your spiritual radar.

Why Did God Allow Us to Disobey and Suffer?
God is love. Love always offers a choice to accept or reject Divine love. If the woman and man cannot freely reject God's offer of life and love, God violates the freedom of the beings made in the Divine image. Yet God would not have allowed this freedom if it would undo his plan for humankind. Our promise is that Jesus' Redemption will open a new heavens and a new earth with more blessing and glory than the first creation.

EXERCISE RECORD

1. When I Awake in the Morning—1 Minute Minimum - 2 Maximum

Location_____ I Exercised Yes___(___Minutes) No____

2. Morning Time Exercise—10 Minutes Minimum -20 Minutes Maximum

Location_____ I Exercised Yes___(___Minutes) No____

3. Examen Exercise Time—15 Minutes Maximum

Location_____ I Exercised Yes___(___Minutes) No____

4. Day Time Exercise—60 Contiguous Minutes (30 or 45 if 60 is not possible)

Location_____ I Exercised Yes___(___Minutes) No____

5. Evening Time Exercise—30 Contiguous Minutes Minimum – 60 Maximum

Location_____ I Exercised Yes___(___Minutes) No____

6. Exercise Journal—1-2 Minutes Once Daily

Location_____ I Exercised Yes___(___Minutes) No____

7. As I Lay Down to Sleep—1 Minute Total

Location_____ I Exercised Yes___(___Minutes) No____

Desolation From the Day – Write no more than two sentences on what decreased your faith, your hope and your love for God and neighbor today.

Consolation From the Day – Write no more than two sentences on what increased your faith, your hope and your love for God and neighbor today.

Week 1

Day Three

Read the following familiar story told in a new way and reflect on the questions.

In the beginning when God created our human nature, the energy field that is our body and spirit was in complete harmony. That perfect balance "created" by God is why we were immortal.

Because God made us in in the Divine image, we had to be free to accept or reject God's gift of love and immortality. The pure spiritual beings in the heavens God created were free to accept or reject God's love.

Some of those spiritual beings did reject God and then sought to destroy God's creation. The main way they could destroy God's creation, they knew, was to corrupt the beings God made in God's likeness. If corrupted, they would be susceptible to destroying each other and creation itself.

The greatest tragedy since the beginning of time is that we succumbed to rejecting God's life and the paradise offered us. At the point of our "original sin", we broke the unified field between spirit and body and we not only lost our innocence but our immortality. From the point of corruption onwards to right now, discernment between what is good and what is evil has become human nature's central challenge.

Spiritual discernment--including developing radar for good and evil--is an essential discipline for us. All of us have felt original sin inside of us. Each of us knows in our heart of hearts that to succumb to temptations is destructive and will not lead to life and light.

If we are to find our way home to our true heart, we must learn to master the spirit-body discipline of spiritual discernment and working ardently to choose God in our thoughts, words and deeds.

Reflection Questions:

What is the first instance I can remember where I was confronted with a choice between good and evil?
What was the context? What did the struggle feel like?
What did I choose?
What were the consequences of my choice?
Write a very short one-paragraph reflection in your Exercise Record about this experience.

EXERCISE RECORD

1. When I Awake in the Morning—1 Minute Minimum - 2 Maximum

Location_____ I Exercised Yes___(___Minutes) No___

2. Morning Time Exercise—10 Minutes Minimum -20 Minutes Maximum

Location_____ I Exercised Yes___(___Minutes) No___

3. Examen Exercise Time—15 Minutes Maximum

Location_____ I Exercised Yes___(___Minutes) No___

4. Day Time Exercise—60 Contiguous Minutes (30 or 45 if 60 is not possible)

Location_____ I Exercised Yes___(___Minutes) No___

5. Evening Time Exercise—30 Contiguous Minutes Minimum – 60 Maximum

Location_____ I Exercised Yes___(___Minutes) No___

6. Exercise Journal—1-2 Minutes Once Daily

Location_____ I Exercised Yes___(___Minutes) No___

7. As I Lay Down to Sleep—1 Minute Total

Location_____ I Exercised Yes___(___Minutes) No___

Desolation From the Day – Write no more than two sentences on what decreased your faith, your hope and your love for God and neighbor today.

Consolation From the Day – Write no more than two sentences on what increased your faith, your hope and your love for God and neighbor today.

WEEK 1

DAY FOUR

Spiritual Exercise for Day or Evening

Go to Daily Mass alone or with a friend or spouse for your Day or Evening time Exercise. Offer the Mass that both you and those close to you can become masters in the art of spiritual discernment.

EXERCISE RECORD

1. When I Awake in the Morning—1 Minute Minimum - 2 Maximum

Location_____ I Exercised Yes___(___Minutes) No___

2. Morning Time Exercise—10 Minutes Minimum -20 Minutes Maximum

Location_____ I Exercised Yes___(___Minutes) No___

3. Examen Exercise Time—15 Minutes Maximum

Location_____ I Exercised Yes___(___Minutes) No___

4. Day Time Exercise—60 Contiguous Minutes (30 or 45 if 60 is not possible)

Location_____ I Exercised Yes___(___Minutes) No___

5. Evening Time Exercise—30 Contiguous Minutes Minimum – 60 Maximum

Location_____ I Exercised Yes___(___Minutes) No___

6. Exercise Journal—1-2 Minutes Once Daily

Location_____ I Exercised Yes___(___Minutes) No___

7. As I Lay Down to Sleep—1 Minute Total

Location_____ I Exercised Yes___(___Minutes) No___

Desolation From the Day – Write no more than two sentences on what decreased your faith, your hope and your love for God and neighbor today.

Consolation From the Day – Write no more than two sentences on what increased your faith, your hope and your love for God and neighbor today.

Week 1

Day Five

Spiritual Exercise for Day or Evening

Read this for your Day or Evening Exercise and reflect on the questions below.

Because we have a human nature that can connect with good or evil spiritual entities, we want to learn how they seek to influence us. Today's Exercise looks at three distinct sources of spiritual "inspirations" that can guide our thoughts, words and deeds.

Saint Ignatius learned about these spiritual sources by careful attention to his affective moods. That is why the Exercises invite you to tune out the electronic world so you can hear the spiritual world. Saint Ignatius learned that spiritual inspirations affecting your human nature (spirit-body) originate from three different sources:

1. Spiritual inspirations can originate from your own life-energy or spirit.
2. Spiritual inspirations can originate from a Divine source: the *Divine-Inspirer*.
3. Spiritual inspirations can originate from a demonic source, the *enemy of human nature*: the *counter-inspirer*.

There are three *sources* of spiritual inspiration, but only two spiritual *states*. St. Ignatius names the two spiritual states *consolation* and *desolation.*

The spiritual inspiration of consolation is when one *experiences*, to a lesser or greater degree, an *increase in faith, hope and love.* The spiritual inspiration of desolation is when one *experiences,* to a lesser or greater degree, *a loss of faith, hope and love.*

Our Quick Review

<u>*Sources of Inspiration*</u>

✠   Human nature as a source of inspiration
✠   God as the *Divine-Inspirer*
✠   The enemy of human nature as the *counter-inspirer*

<u>*Types of Inspiration*</u>

✠   Spiritual Inspiration of Consolation—increase of faith, hope and love
✠   Spiritual Inspiration of Desolation—decrease of faith, hope and love

Reflection Questions

Pray to the Divine-Inspirer to have your memory "energized." Use the name for God-the Divine-Inspirer—you discovered in the introductory Exercises for all your prayers from now on. (Set up this exercise in the introduction).

Ask for the grace to remember one time that your radar picked up the spiritual energy of consolation where you experienced an increase of faith, hope and love. What was the event/experience and what would you guess was the source? REMEMBER!

Next, pray to the Divine Inspirer to have your memory "energized" again. Ask for the grace to remember one time when your radar picked up the spiritual energy of desolation where you had a decrease in faith, hope, or love. What was the event/experience and what would you guess was the source? REMEMBER!

Briefly write one or two sentences in your Exercise Record about each memory that captures the experience and how you felt during these two different "energized states" and the source from which you think they originated.

Example: *Today when I invited Greg to come on the weekend camping trip with our group he realized people care about him. Seeing him smile made me feel great and I knew I had done the right thing. His smile made me feel faith, hope and love. That must have been the Holy Spirit.*

Example: *When Greg asked if he could come with our group on the camping trip I was not honest and told him we had no more room. Seeing his disappointment made me feel bad and my lack of honesty and what it did to him really decreased my faith, hope and love. I must have been tempted to this dishonesty and I know it was not 'of God.'*

EXERCISE RECORD

1. When I Awake in the Morning—1 Minute Minimum - 2 Maximum

Location_____ I Exercised Yes___(___Minutes) No___

2. Morning Time Exercise—10 Minutes Minimum -20 Minutes Maximum

Location_____ I Exercised Yes___(___Minutes) No___

3. Examen Exercise Time—15 Minutes Maximum

Location_____ I Exercised Yes___(___Minutes) No___

4. Day Time Exercise—60 Contiguous Minutes (30 or 45 if 60 is not possible)

Location_____ I Exercised Yes___(___Minutes) No___

5. Evening Time Exercise—30 Contiguous Minutes Minimum – 60 Maximum

Location_____ I Exercised Yes___(___Minutes) No___

6. Exercise Journal—1-2 Minutes Once Daily

Location_____ I Exercised Yes___(___Minutes) No___

7. As I Lay Down to Sleep—1 Minute Total

Location_____ I Exercised Yes___(___Minutes) No___

Desolation From the Day – Write no more than two sentences on what decreased your faith, your hope and your love for God and neighbor today.

Consolation From the Day – Write no more than two sentences on what increased your faith, your hope and your love for God and neighbor today.

Week 1

Day Six

Spiritual Exercise for Day or Evening

I will go for a thirty minute walk or run or find a quiet place to sit where I can see nature. I will not listen to music or bring my cell phone with me. I will listen instead to my daydreams, nature, and the people I pass by. I will notice people who appear happy and those who seem to be struggling. I will listen to and watch the world God made for my enjoyment, appreciation and engagement. I realize that I have spiritual energy that reaches to the end of the cosmos and beyond. I will attune my radar to what is holy and reject what is evil. I will listen to what brings me joy or makes me sad.

At the end of your walk, run or quiet time speak to God from your heart and ask God to help you with the one thing you need most today in developing your spiritual radar.

EXERCISE RECORD

1. When I Awake in the Morning—1 Minute Minimum - 2 Maximum

Location_____ I Exercised Yes____(____Minutes) No____

2. Morning Time Exercise—10 Minutes Minimum -20 Minutes Maximum

Location_____ I Exercised Yes____(____Minutes) No____

3. Examen Exercise Time—15 Minutes Maximum

Location_____ I Exercised Yes____(____Minutes) No____

4. Day Time Exercise—60 Contiguous Minutes (30 or 45 if 60 is not possible)

Location_____ I Exercised Yes____(____Minutes) No____

5. Evening Time Exercise—30 Contiguous Minutes Minimum – 60 Maximum

Location_____ I Exercised Yes____(____Minutes) No____

6. Exercise Journal—1-2 Minutes Once Daily

Location_____ I Exercised Yes____(____Minutes) No____

7. As I Lay Down to Sleep—1 Minute Total

Location_____ I Exercised Yes____(____Minutes) No____

Desolation From the Day – Write no more than two sentences on what decreased your faith, your hope and your love for God and neighbor today.

Consolation From the Day – Write no more than two sentences on what increased your faith, your hope and your love for God and neighbor today.

Week 1

Day Seven

Spiritual Exercise for Day or Evening

Go to Sunday Mass alone or with a friend for your Day or Evening Time exercise. Offer the Mass for the intention that the Church can help everyone in the world to hear and follow the voice of the Divine-Inspirer.

EXERCISE RECORD

1. When I Awake in the Morning—1 Minute Minimum - 2 Maximum

Location_____ I Exercised Yes___(___Minutes) No___

2. Morning Time Exercise—10 Minutes Minimum -20 Minutes Maximum

Location_____ I Exercised Yes___(___Minutes) No___

3. Examen Exercise Time—15 Minutes Maximum

Location_____ I Exercised Yes___(___Minutes) No___

4. Day Time Exercise—60 Contiguous Minutes (30 or 45 if 60 is not possible)

Location_____ I Exercised Yes___(___Minutes) No___

5. Evening Time Exercise—30 Contiguous Minutes Minimum – 60 Maximum

Location_____ I Exercised Yes___(___Minutes) No___

6. Exercise Journal—1-2 Minutes Once Daily

Location_____ I Exercised Yes___(___Minutes) No___

7. As I Lay Down to Sleep—1 Minute Total

Location_____ I Exercised Yes___(___Minutes) No___

8. Night Vigils—30 minutes minimum – 45 maximum

Location_____ I Exercised   Yes___(___Minutes) No___

Desolation From the Day – Write no more than two sentences on what decreased your faith, your hope and your love for God and neighbor today.

Consolation From the Day – Write no more than two sentences on what increased your faith, your hope and your love for God and neighbor today.

NOTES

NOTES

NIGHT VIGIL
WEEK 1

Spend thirty to forty-five minutes on this meditation. Do only one section at a time and do not read ahead. Do not feel compelled to finish the whole sheet. Stay with each section until your heart suggests moving on. Do not read or write after this meditation except perhaps a short journal entry.
Be Alone.

Temptation in the Wilderness

Leopold Marbeouf

I. Gather in what your senses are experiencing. Breathe in the Spirit of God. Breathe out whatever is troubling, distracting, or burdensome. Be aware of all the thoughts and feelings coming from the day so far.

II. Talk to Jesus in your own words about your desire for this particular grace: "that I may come to know and believe God the Father as the source of my greatest freedom and that I may come to understand more clearly the source of my greatest un-freedom (my sense of being in prison)." Stay with this for as long as you like. Don't feel compelled to move on unless your heart suggests.

III. Imagine yourself accompanying Jesus away from the Jordan River, out into the wilderness. This is the first time you have decided to go away, apart from your family and friends. This is your first attempt to spend such a lengthy time in prayer and silence with your God. You are both filled with the Holy Spirit -- yet it is not long before you are faced with the insidious seduction of the spirit of evil and darkness. See and experience the events as they happen. Notice everything about what is happening to Jesus and yourself. Do not move to the next section unless your heart suggests.

Open your Bible and enter the scene of the story in Luke 4: 1-13 See, feel, touch, smell everything about the story because Scripture is a "living word."

IV. ASK THE LORD FOR HIS STRENGTH AND GUIDANCE in facing the temptations and the ways your spirit is not free be a true to your authentic human nature.

-THE BREAD which represents the material possessions and comforts that you feel you need for status and security;

-THE POWER of independence, self-sufficiency and pride which keep you, not God, as the center of your life, for not realizing your need for God as the Source of your freedom and life;

-THE VANITY of self-centeredness which subtly manipulates or exploits others, testing the fidelity of God and others in their love for you.

ASK THE LORD FOR HIS HELP in letting go of what binds you; of what keeps you from freely loving others, from freely giving you heart to God, and from freely being your truest self.

V. Following the meditation, bring your own prayer period to a close by slowly praying the *Our Father,* listening to the words in your heart as you pray. Briefly write any inspirations in your Exercise Record.

Week 2

Day One

Spiritual Exercise for Day or Evening

Read this for your Day or Evening Exercise
and reflect on the questions below.

HOW INSPIRATIONS WORK IN THE "REAL WORLD"

Sources of Spiritual Inspiration

To affirm that our human nature can be the source of inspirations makes perfect sense. We have our own thoughts and convictions and act on them. Such thoughts originate from within our being in several ways.

First, we sometimes let our *body* make decisions. Being led by our sensual appetites, we "give into them" with little or no conscious thought about the consequences. Sometimes that "giving in" is due to sickness or addictions. Every time, however, it is the appetites that we allow to "inspire" our actions.

Second, we can be inspired by the energy of what we might call *embedded strengths/gifts* in human nature from our Creator OR from *embedded diseases/weaknesses* in human nature marred by Original Sin.

Consolation from an *embedded strength/gift* in human nature from our Creator could be a bodily feeling that "life is good" after an excellent workout. It might also be a spiritual feeling of being happy to be alive, that "life is beautiful" when looking at a baby or a beautiful sunset. The overall impact of this spiritual energy is to increase your faith, hope and love.

Desolation from an *embedded disease/weakness* in human nature marred by Original Sin might be a bodily feeling that "life is miserable" when you have a cold, flu or some type of bodily injury. It might also be a spiritual feeling that "life is difficult, burdensome and not fair" if you are hurting in a relationship or suffering from a defeat in some way. The overall impact of this spiritual energy is to decrease your faith, hope and love.

If you are inspired spiritually by either the Divine-Inspirer or the counter-inspirer, the inspirational energy will be communicated to you through your higher spiritual nature which God created to guide your lower physical nature. We will look at this reality in future exercises.

Reflection Questions:

Pray to the Divine-Inspirer to have your memory "energized." Ask for the grace to remember one time that your radar picked up the spiritual energy of *consolation*—the feeling of an increase of faith, hope and love in connection with a physical sense in your body and "life is good."

What was the event/experience and what would you guess was the source? REMEMBER!

Next, pray to the Divine Inspirer to have your memory "energized" again. Ask for the grace to remember one time when your radar picked up the spiritual energy of *desolation*—the feeling of a decrease in faith, hope, or love in connection with a physical sense in your body that "life is difficult, burdensome or not fair."

What was the event/experience and what would you guess was the source? REMEMBER!

Briefly write one or two sentences in your Exercise Record about each memory that captures the experience and how you felt during these two different "energized states."

Example: *We got the job because I made a difficult problem look easy. I felt great because I had worked so hard on it and knew that my example of discipline helped the whole team.*

Example*: We lost the job because I made a difficult problem seem impossible to solve. I felt stupid and ashamed and miserable for many days afterward because I knew how I could have avoided this situation. I just couldn't get over how I let my team down.*

EXERCISE RECORD

1. When I Awake in the Morning—1 Minute Minimum - 2 Maximum

Location_____ I Exercised Yes___(___Minutes) No___

2. Morning Time Exercise—10 Minutes Minimum -20 Minutes Maximum

Location_____ I Exercised Yes___(___Minutes) No___

3. Examen Exercise Time—15 Minutes Maximum

Location_____ I Exercised Yes___(___Minutes) No___

4. Day Time Exercise—60 Contiguous Minutes (30 or 45 if 60 is not possible)

Location_____ I Exercised Yes___(___Minutes) No___

5. Evening Time Exercise—30 Contiguous Minutes Minimum – 60 Maximum

Location_____ I Exercised Yes___(___Minutes) No___

6. Exercise Journal—1-2 Minutes Once Daily

Location_____ I Exercised Yes___(___Minutes) No___

7. As I Lay Down to Sleep—1 Minute Total

Location_____ I Exercised Yes___(___Minutes) No___

Desolation From the Day – Write no more than two sentences on what decreased your faith, your hope and your love for God and neighbor today.

Consolation From the Day – Write no more than two sentences on what increased your faith, your hope and your love for God and neighbor today.

Week 2

Day Two

Spiritual Exercise for Day or Evening Time

Go to Daily Mass alone or with a friend for your Day or Evening Exercise Time. Offer the Mass today in thanksgiving that God has given you spiritual radar and ask God for help to use it in your daily life.

EXERCISE RECORD

1. When I Awake in the Morning—1 Minute Minimum - 2 Maximum

Location_____   I Exercised Yes___(___Minutes) No___

2. Morning Time Exercise—10 Minutes Minimum -20 Minutes Maximum

Location_____   I Exercised Yes___(___Minutes) No___

3. Examen Exercise Time—15 Minutes Maximum

Location_____   I Exercised Yes___(___Minutes) No___

4. Day Time Exercise—60 Contiguous Minutes (30 or 45 if 60 is not possible)

Location_____   I Exercised Yes___(___Minutes) No___

5. Evening Time Exercise—30 Contiguous Minutes Minimum – 60 Maximum

Location_____   I Exercised Yes___(___Minutes) No___

6. Exercise Journal—1-2 Minutes Once Daily

Location_____   I Exercised Yes___(___Minutes) No___

7. As I Lay Down to Sleep—1 Minute Total

Location_____   I Exercised Yes___(___Minutes) No___

Desolation From the Day – Write no more than two sentences on what decreased your faith, your hope and your love for God and neighbor today.

Consolation From the Day – Write no more than two sentences on what increased your faith, your hope and your love for God and neighbor today.

Week 2

Day Three

Spiritual Exercise for Day or Evening

Read this for your Day or Evening Exercise and reflect on the questions below.

WE WERE CREARTED IMMORTAL AND
THE CHRISTIAN LIFE IS A PATH BACK TO
A FUTURE PARADISE AND IMMORTALITY!

Below is a brief review of some past Exercises on the nature of the "real world" –the Spiritual World.

God willed that human nature be a perfect unity of body and soul. The gift of this blessed unity of human nature completely at one with God in paradise made us immortal. The turning from God, which we call Original Sin, was a sin of our spiritual nature. This sin broke the perfect unity of human nature: body and soul. As a result, a battle begins where the spirit and body are divided opening up human nature to every form of corruption, bodily and spiritual.

In this battle our authentic identity was distorted. Our conscience was clouded and we lost sight of right and wrong. Disease, strife, suffering and death resulted. Original Sin broke our perfect unity with God's loving will. Also broken was the unity between male and female and their harmony with creation. Paradise was an ecstasy of harmonious relationships. Original Sin broke all relationships and for beings made in the Divine image, it broke our hearts. But God had a rescue plan.

The plan begins with God choosing a people to reunite human hearts to God. To do that, what constitutes "right relationship" based on our Divinely crafted human nature had to be "revealed" to people who lost sight of all truth. The revelation of the Ten Commandments to the people of Israel was one of the most significant gifts from God. God gave the Ten Commandments to help us re-learn "right relationship." The Decalogue prepared the Chosen People to be the source from which the Messiah would become flesh.

In the New Covenant, Jesus Christ is the ultimate revelation of God— "The Word became flesh and dwelt among us" (Jn 1:14). Christ's life and message is the most perfect expression of how each of us is called to live and is the fulfillment of the Covenant made to the people of Israel to restore all things—leading to a new heaves and a new earth. In Christ, we have the forgiveness of sins which heals our souls and opens back the path to eternity.

Our Judeo/Christian heritage is a "revealed religion." How important this is! We did not come to the truth by our own reasoning processes. It had to be revealed to us by God and mediated to us first by the Chosen people and the prophets of the Old Testament and then through Christ and the body that becomes His people—the Church. This teaching Church has been entrusted with interpreting, passing on and holding secure for all people the authentic message of Christ and the revealed Truths of God and our own Divinely crafted human nature.

This is the same Church that Ignatius served and loved. His discernment principles are spiritual guidelines that help us understand the revealed truth of "right relationship" in our own lives according to the revealed truths entrusted to the teaching Church. The "rules" were given as gift and we want to follow them so right relationships can guide and protect our lives crafted in the Divine image.

Ignatius' discernment" rules" are discovered when you begin to pay close attention to inspirations-energy that we identify through *affective feelings*—our inner feelings and thoughts. We are "inspired" in thoughts, emotions, words and deeds from three sources:

✠ our own human nature (body and soul);
✠ the Divine-Inspirer;
✠ and human nature's enemy, the counter-inspirer.

These "inspirations" have one of two effects on us, they either create spiritual consolation (an increase of faith, hope or love) or spiritual desolation (decrease in faith, hope or love). In our next exercise we begin looking at these two types of inspiration-energy more in-depth.

Reflection Questions:

Have you ever reflected on the truth that God created us immortal and that immortality was lost due to sin? Do you believe this? If so why-if not why?

Do you believe the Commandments and the teachings of Christ are gifts to protect and guide your heart to find its ultimate meaning and happiness? If so why-if not why?

Write some short responses in the NOTES section to each of these questions.

EXERCISE RECORD

1. When I Awake in the Morning—1 Minute Minimum - 2 Maximum

Location_____ I Exercised Yes___(___Minutes) No____

2. Morning Time Exercise—10 Minutes Minimum -20 Minutes Maximum

Location_____ I Exercised Yes___(___Minutes) No____

3. Examen Exercise Time—15 Minutes Maximum

Location_____ I Exercised Yes___(___Minutes) No____

4. Day Time Exercise—60 Contiguous Minutes (30 or 45 if 60 is not possible)

Location_____ I Exercised Yes___(___Minutes) No____

5. Evening Time Exercise—30 Contiguous Minutes Minimum – 60 Maximum

Location_____ I Exercised Yes___(___Minutes) No____

6. Exercise Journal—1-2 Minutes Once Daily

Location_____ I Exercised Yes___(___Minutes) No____

7. As I Lay Down to Sleep—1 Minute Total

Location_____ I Exercised Yes___(___Minutes) No____

Desolation From the Day – <u>Write no more than two sentences</u> on what decreased your faith, your hope and your love for God and neighbor today.

Consolation From the Day – <u>Write no more than two sentences</u> on what increased your faith, your hope and your love for God and neighbor today.

Week 2

Day Four

Spiritual Exercise for Day or Evening

I will go for a thirty minute walk or run or find a quiet place to sit where I can see nature. I will not listen to music or bring my cell phone with me. I will listen instead to my daydreams, nature, and the people I pass by. I will notice people who appear happy and those who seem to be struggling. I will listen to and watch the world God made for my enjoyment, appreciation and engagement. I realize that I have spiritual energy that reaches to the end of the cosmos and beyond. I will attune my radar to what is holy and reject what is evil. I will listen to what brings me joy or makes me sad.

At the end of your walk, run or quiet time speak to God from your heart and ask God to help you with the one thing you need most today in developing your spiritual radar.

EXERCISE RECORD

1. When I Awake in the Morning—1 Minute Minimum - 2 Maximum

Location_____   I Exercised Yes___(___Minutes) No___

2. Morning Time Exercise—10 Minutes Minimum -20 Minutes Maximum

Location_____   I Exercised Yes___(___Minutes) No___

3. Examen Exercise Time—15 Minutes Maximum

Location_____   I Exercised Yes___(___Minutes) No___

4. Day Time Exercise—60 Contiguous Minutes (30 or 45 if 60 is not possible)

Location_____   I Exercised Yes___(___Minutes) No___

5. Evening Time Exercise—30 Contiguous Minutes Minimum – 60 Maximum

Location_____   I Exercised Yes___(___Minutes) No___

6. Exercise Journal—1-2 Minutes Once Daily

Location_____   I Exercised Yes___(___Minutes) No___

7. As I Lay Down to Sleep—1 Minute Total

Location_____   I Exercised Yes___(___Minutes) No___

Desolation From the Day – Write no more than two sentences on what decreased your faith, your hope and your love for God and neighbor today.

Consolation From the Day – Write no more than two sentences on what increased your faith, your hope and your love for God and neighbor today.

Week 2

Day Five

Spiritual Exercise for Day or Evening

Read this for your Day or Evening Exercise
and reflect on the questions below.

*WE CAN COLLABORATE
WITH SPIRITUAL ENTITIES THAT LEAD US
TO AN IMMORTALITY OF FREINDSHIP AND JOY
OR AN IMMORTALITY OF LONELINESS AND DESPAIR*

*GOD HAS GIVEN US SPIRITUAL RADAR TO HELP US
FOLLOW THE PATH TO ETERNAL JOY
AND REJECT THE PATH OF ETERNAL LONLINESS*

YOU HAVE A RADAR FOR JOY

First Benchmark Strategy for Spiritual Discernment

To help your awakening and initiation into spiritual discernment, two benchmark guidelines will be beneficial in many life situations. You have already been exposed to them in your life, but now you will focus on them more consciously.

As I lead you in this work I want to speak a truth it has taken me a long time to accept: Divine inspiration, or consolation, does not always *feel good*. It is hard work sometimes. It feels like a struggle sometimes. That is okay.

Equally important is to realize that an unholy inspiration, or spiritual desolation, does not always *feel bad*. Temptation and evil can, strangely, feel good. That is not okay.

We will explore this seeming paradox in a later exercise.

For now it is sufficient to reflect on the two principal benchmark guidelines. Understood and followed, they will help you direct your authentic human nature towards God and away from human nature's enemy in thoughts, words and deeds.

Benchmark One: Authentic divine energy-inspirations called consolations will have specific features. Consolations will:

1) increase your heart's love for God, family, and others

2) increase the virtues of humility and self-generosity

3) not oppose the truths and teachings of Scripture, the Tradition and the teaching Church.

Consolation can be the consequence of the Divine Physician's Spirit working in you. This form of consolation helps strengthen your heart and soul, encouraging you to turn to God whenever you need spiritual and moral help. Consolation helps you to choose thoughts, words and deeds that express your authentic human nature—your truest self—made in the Divine image.

Consolation can also be the result of your Divinely-shaped human nature expressing itself through your daily life. God created your human nature as a gift in the Divine image and likeness. In spite of Original Sin's impact, cooperating with God's grace activates embedded life forces of your Divinely-shaped human nature. These imbedded strengths can help you heal biochemically, strengthen your immune system and reset physiological and emotional imbalances; energize you; and enable thoughts, words and deeds that express your authentic human nature.

Reflection Questions

Pray to the Divine-Inspirer to have your memory "energized." Ask for the grace to remember one time that your love for God and/or other people was stirred in you. What was the context? Remember and briefly write the context and experience in your journal.

Example: "I remember on a retreat we had a Mass that made me feel a part of not just the retreat group, but something much bigger. That to me was a time I really felt God and really felt great about the whole world."

Then ask for the grace to remember one time that you were inspired to be more humble and giving of yourself to others. What as the context? Remember and briefly write the context and experience in your journal.

Example: *I remember when I won a contest and my closest friend lost. I knew how I would feel if I had lost and I asked them to share the prize with me.*

Ask for the grace to remember one time when you were inspired to follow the teachings of the Scriptures, Catholic Tradition or the Church that stirred your faith, hope and love. What was the context? Remember and briefly write the context and experience in your journal.

Example: *I read an article about how marital fidelity strengthens both husband and wife and gives children more hope and security in support of Church teachings on marriage. I decided that I would make fidelity a conscious spiritual goal for my life and to pray that this gift would be given to us in our family.*

EXERCISE RECORD

1. When I Awake in the Morning—1 Minute Minimum - 2 Maximum

Location_____ I Exercised Yes___(___Minutes) No___

2. Morning Time Exercise—10 Minutes Minimum -20 Minutes Maximum

Location_____ I Exercised Yes___(___Minutes) No___

3. Examen Exercise Time—15 Minutes Maximum

Location_____ I Exercised Yes___(___Minutes) No___

4. Day Time Exercise—60 Contiguous Minutes (30 or 45 if 60 is not possible)

Location_____ I Exercised Yes___(___Minutes) No___

5. Evening Time Exercise—30 Contiguous Minutes Minimum – 60 Maximum

Location_____ I Exercised Yes___(___Minutes) No___

6. Exercise Journal—1-2 Minutes Once Daily

Location_____ I Exercised Yes___(___Minutes) No___

7. As I Lay Down to Sleep—1 Minute Total

Location_____ I Exercised Yes___(___Minutes) No___

Desolation From the Day – Write no more than two sentences on what decreased your faith, your hope and your love for God and neighbor today.

Consolation From the Day – Write no more than two sentences on what increased your faith, your hope and your love for God and neighbor today.

WEEK 2

DAY SIX

Spiritual Exercise for Day or Evening

I will go for a thirty minute walk or run or find a quiet place to sit where I can see nature. I will not listen to music or bring my cell phone with me. I will listen instead to my daydreams, nature, and the people who pass by. I will notice people who appear happy and those who seem to be struggling. I will listen to and watch the world God made for my enjoyment, appreciation and engagement. I realize that I have spiritual energy that reaches to the end of the cosmos and beyond. I will attune my radar to what is holy and reject what is evil. I will listen to what brings me joy or makes me sad.

At the end of your walk, run or quiet time speak to God from your heart and ask God to help you with the one thing you need most today in developing your spiritual radar.

EXERCISE RECORD

1. When I Awake in the Morning—1 Minute Minimum - 2 Maximum

Location_____ I Exercised Yes___(___Minutes) No____

2. Morning Time Exercise—10 Minutes Minimum -20 Minutes Maximum

Location_____ I Exercised Yes___(___Minutes) No____

3. Examen Exercise Time—15 Minutes Maximum

Location_____ I Exercised Yes___(___Minutes) No____

4. Day Time Exercise—60 Contiguous Minutes (30 or 45 if 60 is not possible)

Location_____ I Exercised Yes___(___Minutes) No____

5. Evening Time Exercise—30 Contiguous Minutes Minimum – 60 Maximum

Location_____ I Exercised Yes___(___Minutes) No____

6. Exercise Journal—1-2 Minutes Once Daily

Location_____ I Exercised Yes___(___Minutes) No____

7. As I Lay Down to Sleep—1 Minute Total

Location_____ I Exercised Yes___(___Minutes) No____

Desolation From the Day – Write no more than two sentences on what decreased your faith, your hope and your love for God and neighbor today.

Consolation From the Day – Write no more than two sentences on what increased your faith, your hope and your love for God and neighbor today.

WEEK 2

DAY SEVEN

Read this for your Day or Evening Exercise
and reflect on the questions below

We can collaborate with spiritual entities that lead us to an immortality of friendship and joy or an immortality of loneliness and despair. God has given us spiritual radar to follow the path to eternal joy and life and reject the path of eternal loneliness and death.

YOU HAVE A RADAR FOR LONELINESS

Second Benchmark Guideline for Spiritual Discernment

This benchmark deals with counter energy-inspirations that come from the enemy of human nature. These, if followed, ultimately lead to eternal loneliness.

Benchmark Two: Authentic counter-inspirations called desolations will have specific features. Desolations will:

1) increase narcissism, displacing God and others from your heart

2) decrease obedience and humility, and increase pride and self-satisfaction

3) arouse hungers and desires that, although they feel good, will typically contradict the truths and teachings proposed by the Scripture, Tradition, and the teaching Church.

The author of counter-inspirations is opposed to Christ and will lead you away from life and truth. Counter-inspirations will produce desires *that feel authentic* because they are linked to *fallen* human nature's physical lusts and spiritual pride. They are the familiar default drives of a broken heart and a human nature and conscience darkened by sin.

Desolation can be the consequence of the enemy of human nature working in you. This form of desolation helps weaken your heart and soul, encouraging you to turn from God. Desolation helps you choose thoughts, words and deeds that are opposed to your Divinely-shaped human nature—your truest self.

Desolation can also be the consequence of your own fallen human nature. God created your human nature as a gift in the Divine image and likeness. Yet, because of Original Sin's impact, not cooperating with God's grace erodes embedded life forces of your Divinely-shaped human nature, helping to weaken your immune system and undermine biochemical, physiological, emotional and spiritual balance; de-energizing you; and increasing thoughts, words and deeds that are in opposition to your authentic human nature—your truest self.

Reflection Questions

Pray to the Divine-Inspirer to have your memory "energized." Ask for the grace to remember one time when your love for God and/or other people was diminished in favor of more selfish acts or inspirations. What was the context? Remember and briefly write the context and experience in your journal.

Example: "I remember on retreat we had a Mass that made me feel left out because not chosen as to share my share my spiritual insights. I was angry about that and did not participate because of it."

Ask for the grace to remember one time that you were inspired to be less humble and giving of yourself to others. What as the context? Remember and briefly write the context and experience in your journal.

Example: *I remember when I won a contest and my closest lost. I knew how I would feel if I lost but was really glad I won. I could have shared the prize with my friend but chose to keep it all for myself.*

Ask for the grace to remember one time when you were inspired by hungers and desires not follow the teachings of the Scriptures, Catholic Tradition or the Church. What was the context? Remember and briefly write the context and experience in your journal.

Example: *I read an article about how marital fidelity strengthens both husband and wife and gives children more hope and security in support of Church teachings on marriage. I decided that I did not want to be ridiculed for openly speaking about this in our current divorce culture so I did not talk about it with anyone.*

EXERCISE RECORD

1. When I Awake in the Morning—1 Minute Minimum - 2 Maximum

Location_____ I Exercised Yes____(____Minutes) No____

2. Morning Time Exercise—10 Minutes Minimum -20 Minutes Maximum

Location_____ I Exercised Yes____(____Minutes) No____

3. Examen Exercise Time—15 Minutes Maximum

Location_____ I Exercised Yes____(____Minutes) No____

4. Day Time Exercise—60 Contiguous Minutes (30 or 45 if 60 is not possible)

Location_____ I Exercised Yes____(____Minutes) No____

5. Evening Time Exercise—30 Contiguous Minutes Minimum – 60 Maximum

Location_____ I Exercised Yes____(____Minutes) No____

6. Exercise Journal—1-2 Minutes Once Daily

Location_____ I Exercised Yes____(____Minutes) No____

7. As I Lay Down to Sleep—1 Minute Total

Location_____ I Exercised Yes____(____Minutes) No____

8. Night Vigils—30 minutes minimum – 45 maximum

Location_____ I Exercised Yes____(____Minutes) No____

Desolation From the Day – Write no more than two sentences on what decreased your faith, your hope and your love for God and neighbor today.

Consolation From the Day – Write no more than two sentences on what increased your faith, your hope and your love for God and neighbor today.

NOTES

NOTES

NIGHT VIGIL
WEEK 2

THE RICH YOUNG MAN

Now that you are reflecting more intentionally on the "real world—"the spiritual world", this Gospel will take on new meaning. As you read, notice how this story is about your growing and maturing radar as a Christian— radar for both friendship and loneliness.

Notice how you have radar for following the joy in your heart, too, though sometimes you "choose" loneliness instead of friendship. We all stopped short of surrendering what holds us back from the love and life of our truest heart's most deep desire. How subtle is the work of the counter-inspirer and how many

Rich Young Man

Leopold Marbeouf

are tricked by him! Pray with the Triple Colloquy below first for the grace to develop your radar. If you have time, do the Gospel meditation as well.

Spend thirty to forty-five minutes on this meditation. Be open to all thoughts, feelings, and ideas you have coming from the day. Spend some time talking with God about the things you think significant. Stay here as long as you are comfortable. **Be Alone.**

I. Begin this meditation by asking Jesus to be with you. Ask Jesus to give you the graces he feels will be best for you during this time of the retreat and this time of prayer. Specifically ask for the grace to know the good you desire and how you can be tempted to choose things in life that don't bring you peace and happiness. Use the *Triple Colloquy* below to ask for these graces. Then do the meditation below.

II. Open your Bible to the tenth chapter of Mark, verses seventeen through thirty-one. Before you read, plan to read it slowly so you can visualize the scenes as they really happened; only place yourself in the crowd. Notice all the details of the people, the smells, the sounds, etc. Keep aware of all the thoughts and feelings you had entering this meditation but now also focus on the events as they unfold before you.

* What is the dilemma of this person? Can you sense what he may be feeling as he speaks to Jesus and asks him the questions he does? What is the man really looking for? Why does he leave in such a sad state of mind? Stop the man and ask him what he is thinking and feeling as he leaves Jesus. What does he say?

III. Pay attention to your reaction to the events that have unfolded before you. See the man leave the presence of Jesus. Walk up to Jesus from your place in the crowd. You are present before Jesus so no one else in the crowd can hear you. Speak to Jesus about what you have just seen and heard. What do you say? What does Jesus say?

IV. Ask Jesus if there is anything in your own life that would prevent you from being his disciple. Ask Jesus about any particular things in your own life that you think may cause you to walk away sadly from him like the person you just witnessed. What is Jesus' response to your question? Stop and listen. What are you thinking and feeling?

V. Pray: *Take, Lord, and receive all my liberty, my memory, my understanding, and my entire will; all that I have and possess. You have given all to me. To you, Lord, I return it. Everything is yours; dispose of it according to your will. Give me only your love and your grace. That is enough for me. Amen!*

TRIPLE COLLOQUY OF SAINT IGNATIUS

First Colloquy, or conversation, will be with Mary. Speak with Mary, using your own words asking her to obtain from her Son the grace to choose what brings peace and happiness and avoid what brings the opposite. When you finish this conversation, pray the *Hail Mary* slowly, thinking of the words and the person to whom you are praying.

Hail Mary, full of grace, The Lord is with thee.
Blessed art thou amongst women
and blessed is the fruit of thy womb, Jesus.
Holy Mary, Mother of God, Pray for us sinners,
now and at the hour of our death. Amen.

Second Colloquy, or conversation, will be with Jesus. Speak directly to Jesus, asking him to request his Father for the same graces as above. When you finish your conversation, pray the *Anima Christi* slowly, thinking of the words and the person to whom you are praying.

Soul of Christ, sanctify me. Body of Christ, save me.
Blood of Christ, inebriate me. Water from the side of Christ wash me.
Passion of Christ, strengthen me. O Good Jesus, hear me. Within thy
wounds, hide me. Permit me not to be separated from thee. From the
wicked foe, defend me. At the hour of my death, call me, And bid me
come to thee that with thy saints I may praise thee forever and ever.
Amen.

Third Colloquy, or conversation, will be with God the Father. Ask the Father directly in your own words to give you the graces you have asked for above. When you finish, pray the *Our Father*, thinking of the words and the person to whom you are praying.

Our Father, Who art in heaven, hallowed be thy name.
Thy Kingdom come, Thy will be done, on earth as it is in heaven. Give us
this day our daily bread, and forgive us our trespasses, As we forgive
those who trespass against us.
Lead us not into temptation, but deliver us from evil.
Amen.

Week 3

Day One

Spiritual Exercise for Day or Evening

I will go to Daily Mass alone or with friend during my Day or Evening Exercise Time. I will offer my Mass today for the person who has been on my mind the most these past few days.

EXERCISE RECORD

1. When I Awake in the Morning—1 Minute Minimum - 2 Maximum

Location_____ I Exercised Yes___(___Minutes) No____

2. Morning Time Exercise—10 Minutes Minimum -20 Minutes Maximum

Location_____ I Exercised Yes___(___Minutes) No____

3. Examen Exercise Time—15 Minutes Maximum

Location_____ I Exercised Yes___(___Minutes) No____

4. Day Time Exercise—60 Contiguous Minutes (30 or 45 if 60 is not possible)

Location_____ I Exercised Yes___(___Minutes) No____

5. Evening Time Exercise—30 Contiguous Minutes Minimum – 60 Maximum

Location_____ I Exercised Yes___(___Minutes) No____

6. Exercise Journal—1-2 Minutes Once Daily

Location_____ I Exercised Yes___(___Minutes) No____

7. As I Lay Down to Sleep—1 Minute Total

Location_____ I Exercised Yes___(___Minutes) No____

Desolation From the Day – Write no more than two sentences on what decreased your faith, your hope and your love for God and neighbor today.

Consolation From the Day – Write no more than two sentences on what increased your faith, your hope and your love for God and neighbor today.

Week 3

Day Two

Spiritual Exercise for Day or Evening

Read this for your Day or Evening Exercise
and reflect on the questions below.

RADAR SIGNALS FROM EITHER THE DIVINE INSPIRER
OR THE COUNTER-INSPIRER
ACT AS HOMING BEACONS FOR YOUR HEART
TO CAUSE THOUGHTS AND FEELINGS OF HOPE OR HOPELESSNESS

For your exercise day or evening time, read and reflect on this exercise in discernment. Pay attention to your moods and *feel* the states of consolation and desolation in your heart. This process requires a *graced awakening*, so as you read this, please ask God for the "eyes to see" your story through the lens of these spiritual lessons. Be patient as you slowly learn this way of understanding your story.

You have learned already that there are three distinct sources influencing your thoughts, words, and deeds. Your own spirit and the Divine-Inspirer and the counter-inspirer. We focus today on the two latter sources.

Both God and the enemy of human nature are aware of your strengths and weaknesses, wounded memories, your hope and hopelessness, your dreams, and fears. God will build on your strengths, inflaming your holy desires, healing what is hurt and broken, and offering eternal friendship to you.

The counter-inspirer—the enemy of human nature—seeks to silence your conscience and hide it in shadows. He will work to magnify your problems, diminish your holy desires and inspire a path that leads to hopelessness and loneliness.

You can identify and distinguish Divine inspirations from counter inspirations by their *intellectual* and *affective* traits, or signature characteristics: *consolation and* desolation.

Reflection Questions:

Pray to the Divine-Inspirer to have your memory "energized." Ask for the grace to remember one time that you are convinced your received a Divine inspiration that filled you with hope and deepened your love for God and strengthened your commitment to your Catholic faith. Remember. What was the context? Briefly describe the context and experience in your journal.

Example: *I remember during a hard time last year I went to Sunday Mass and heard the Gospel story of Jesus healing people. I had a dream that night that everything would work out for the best. When I woke up I had chills because I knew God had helped me and I was not afraid anymore and realized how important my Catholic faith is to my life.*

Pray to the Divine-Inspirer to have your memory "energized." Ask for the grace to remember one time that you are convinced you received a counter-inspiration that seemed right initially but later diminished your love for God and weakened your commitment to your Catholic faith. Remember. What as the context? Briefly describe the context and experience in your journal.

Example: *I remember during a hard time last year I decided it would be best to miss Sunday Mass so I could go for a run and clear my head. It seemed like the right thing at the time, but later I realized it was a mistake because I did not feel better but more confused. It would have been better to go to Mass and let God help me instead of trying to do it all by myself. I went to confession for missing Mass on Sunday and learned a very valuable spiritual lesson.*

EXERCISE RECORD

1. When I Awake in the Morning—1 Minute Minimum - 2 Maximum

Location_____   I Exercised Yes____(____Minutes) No____

2. Morning Time Exercise—10 Minutes Minimum -20 Minutes Maximum

Location_____   I Exercised Yes____(____Minutes) No____

3. Examen Exercise Time—15 Minutes Maximum

Location_____   I Exercised Yes____(____Minutes) No____

4. Day Time Exercise—60 Contiguous Minutes (30 or 45 if 60 is not possible)

Location_____   I Exercised Yes____(____Minutes) No____

5. Evening Time Exercise—30 Contiguous Minutes Minimum – 60 Maximum

Location_____   I Exercised Yes____(____Minutes) No____

6. Exercise Journal—1-2 Minutes Once Daily

Location_____   I Exercised Yes____(____Minutes) No____

7. As I Lay Down to Sleep—1 Minute Total

Location_____   I Exercised Yes____(____Minutes) No____

Desolation From the Day – Write no more than two sentences on what decreased your faith, your hope and your love for God and neighbor today.

Consolation From the Day – Write no more than two sentences on what increased your faith, your hope and your love for God and neighbor today.

Week 3

Day Three

Spiritual Exercise for Day or Evening

I will go for a thirty minute walk or run or find a quiet place to sit where I can see nature. I will not listen to music or bring my cell phone with me. I will listen instead to my daydreams, nature, and the people I pass by. I will notice people who appear happy and those who seem to be struggling. I will listen to and watch the world God made for my enjoyment, appreciation and engagement. I realize that I have spiritual energy that reaches to the end of the cosmos and beyond. I will attune my radar to what is holy and reject what is evil. I will listen to what brings me joy or makes me sad.

At the end of your walk, run or quiet time speak to God from your heart and ask God to help you with the one thing you need most today in developing your spiritual radar.

EXERCISE RECORD

1. When I Awake in the Morning—1 Minute Minimum - 2 Maximum

Location_____ I Exercised Yes____(____Minutes) No____

2. Morning Time Exercise—10 Minutes Minimum -20 Minutes Maximum

Location_____ I Exercised Yes____(____Minutes) No____

3. Examen Exercise Time—15 Minutes Maximum

Location_____ I Exercised Yes____(____Minutes) No____

4. Day Time Exercise—60 Contiguous Minutes (30 or 45 if 60 is not possible)

Location_____ I Exercised Yes____(____Minutes) No____

5. Evening Time Exercise—30 Contiguous Minutes Minimum – 60 Maximum

Location_____ I Exercised Yes____(____Minutes) No____

6. Exercise Journal—1-2 Minutes Once Daily

Location_____ I Exercised Yes____(____Minutes) No____

7. As I Lay Down to Sleep—1 Minute Total

Location_____ I Exercised Yes____(____Minutes) No____

Desolation From the Day – Write no more than two sentences on what decreased your faith, your hope and your love for God and neighbor today.

Consolation From the Day – Write no more than two sentences on what increased your faith, your hope and your love for God and neighbor today.

WEEK 3

DAY FOUR

Spiritual Exercise for Day or Evening

Read this for your Day or Evening Exercise
and reflect on the questions below.

*RADAR SIGNALS FROM
THE DIVINE-INSPIRER OR THE COUNTER-INSPIRER
ACT AS HOMING BEACONS FOR YOUR HEART.
THEY "INSPIRE ACTION AND MOVEMENT"
TOWARDS ONE OF TWO GOALS:*

*JOY, FRIENDSHIP AND SELFLESSNESS
OR
SADNESS, LONELINESS AND SELFISHNESS*

Divine Inspiration: Because consolation defines the feelings and thoughts of a healing heart returning to God and/or residing in God, God is always trying to inspire movement towards reconciliation and union inside your heart.

The signature characteristics of Divine Inspiration include being passionate for God and loving all things in God; tears of remorse and sadness when you fail, yet feeling loved by God despite your failures.

You may experience tears of love for Christ who suffered the consequences of all sin, including your own.

Every increase in love, hope and faith can magnetize your heart towards holy things; and all experiences of peace and quiet in the presence of your Creator. The Divine inspiration of consolation is manifest in humility that views eternal life, lasting love, and faith in God as the hope of the single-hearted, and the ultimate goal of those "willing to risk seeing reality as it truly is."

Counter Inspiration: Desolation defines feelings and thoughts that are the direct opposite of consolation's Divine inspiration. The signature characteristics of counter inspiration are darkness and confusion of a broken and wounded heart, soul, and spirit; magnetic and compulsive attractions to sensual and base appetites; restlessness, anger, cynicism, and temptations that make all things geared towards faith, hope and love appear dull, absurd and even destructive to your heart.

In desolation, you will feel a lazy, lukewarm and sad spirit as if separated from God. Desolation, that painful counter-inspiration, is manifest in everything that magnetizes a broken heart towards cynicism, lusts, isolation, anger, despair and aloneness. It manifests in an unyielding pride that views eternal life, lasting love, and faith in God as beliefs only of the naive. Desolation tempts us to become one of those people, afraid of being healed or happy, who are unwilling to risk seeing reality as truly it is.

Reflection Questions

Pray to the Divine-Inspirer to have your memory "energized." Ask for the grace to remember a whole period in your life that matched the description of Divine Inspiration as consolation. Remember. What was the context? Briefly describe the context and experience in your journal.

Example: *When my baby sister was born I couldn't take my eyes off her. She was such a miracle. I felt like I was in heaven and understood God's holy plan for us.*

Pray to the Divine-Inspirer to have your memory "energized." Ask for the grace to a whole period in your life that matched the description of counter inspiration as desolation. Remember. What as the context? Briefly describe the context and experience in your journal.

Example: *I remember when I got into a fight with my best friend. We hated each other and I felt like I had blown it forever, like I was a terrible person and wouldn't ever have a good friend again. It made me stop praying.*

EXERCISE RECORD

1. When I Awake in the Morning—1 Minute Minimum - 2 Maximum

Location_____ I Exercised Yes___(___Minutes) No___

2. Morning Time Exercise—10 Minutes Minimum -20 Minutes Maximum

Location_____ I Exercised Yes___(___Minutes) No___

3. Examen Exercise Time—15 Minutes Maximum

Location_____ I Exercised Yes___(___Minutes) No___

4. Day Time Exercise—60 Contiguous Minutes (30 or 45 if 60 is not possible)

Location_____ I Exercised Yes___(___Minutes) No___

5. Evening Time Exercise—30 Contiguous Minutes Minimum – 60 Maximum

Location_____ I Exercised Yes___(___Minutes) No___

6. Exercise Journal—1-2 Minutes Once Daily

Location_____ I Exercised Yes___(___Minutes) No___

7. As I Lay Down to Sleep—1 Minute Total

Location_____ I Exercised Yes___(___Minutes) No___

Desolation From the Day – Write no more than two sentences on what decreased your faith, your hope and your love for God and neighbor today.

Consolation From the Day – Write no more than two sentences on what increased your faith, your hope and your love for God and neighbor today.

Week 3

Day Five

Spiritual Exercise for Day or Evening

I will go to Mass alone or with a friend during my Day or Evening Exercise Time. I will offer my Mass today so that I learn what consolation and desolation feel like in my life.

EXERCISE RECORD

1. When I Awake in the Morning—1 Minute Minimum - 2 Maximum

Location_____ I Exercised Yes___(___Minutes) No___

2. Morning Time Exercise—10 Minutes Minimum -20 Minutes Maximum

Location_____ I Exercised Yes___(___Minutes) No___

3. Examen Exercise Time—15 Minutes Maximum

Location_____ I Exercised Yes___(___Minutes) No___

4. Day Time Exercise—60 Contiguous Minutes (30 or 45 if 60 is not possible)

Location_____ I Exercised Yes___(___Minutes) No___

5. Evening Time Exercise—30 Contiguous Minutes Minimum – 60 Maximum

Location_____ I Exercised Yes___(___Minutes) No___

6. Exercise Journal—1-2 Minutes Once Daily

Location_____ I Exercised Yes___(___Minutes) No___

7. As I Lay Down to Sleep—1 Minute Total

Location_____ I Exercised Yes___(___Minutes) No___

Desolation From the Day – Write no more than two sentences on what decreased your faith, your hope and your love for God and neighbor today.

Consolation From the Day – Write no more than two sentences on what increased your faith, your hope and your love for God and neighbor today.

Week 3

Day Six

Spiritual Exercise for Day or Evening

Read this for your Day or Evening Exercise
and reflect on the questions below.

RADAR SIGNALS FROM THE DIVINE INSPIRER
OR THE COUNTER-INSPIRER
CAN BOTH MAKE YOU "FEEL GOOD" OR "FEEL BAD"
AND YOU HAVE TO LEARN HOW TO DECODE THEM

If you are accustomed to physical pleasures, lifestyles, and relationships that fall outside the boundaries of the Commandments and/or Church teaching, the inspiration to cut loose from those pleasures can make you feel distress and anxiety. Remember that Ignatius panicked and felt distress when he realized that he would have to live for the rest of his life without the tempting pleasures of his first thirty years.

Like Ignatius, we can each feel this distress because we are uncertain of what lies beyond the false definition of success and happiness. When we stray away from our truest self or don't know it yet, the future feels like a frightening void.

So the fear aroused in you by the invitation to live authentically needs to be strongly confronted, because you are being invited towards life, not death. Gradually you will learn to resist the fear when moving toward authenticity. There is no courage like this kind of spiritual courage! The success of the rest of our lives depends on it.

Reflection Questions

Pray to the Divine-Inspirer to have your memory "energized." Ask for the grace to remember a time in your life when you confronted fear and found consolation. Remember. Briefly describe the context and experience in your journal.

Example: *In my twenties, I got involved in activities that I was shocked at because I was always a fairly moral person. I did not want to keep losing myself in false pleasures so I broke through my fear and got some help. I was scared at first to let go of my escapes and only felt it would make things worse. But as I challenged and acted against my fear I started to feel hopeful again and unafraid.*

Pray to the Divine-Inspirer to have your memory "energized." Ask for the grace to a time in your life that matched the description of counter inspiration as desolation. Remember. What was the context? Briefly describe the context and experience in your journal.

Example: *I interviewed for a job and was convinced by the response of the team that I was a shoe-in for the position. I was so excited. When they called and told they offered it to someone else I got so depressed. I was convinced for the longest time there was something wrong with me and I was not any good. I then realized how the thoughts were making me feel and I knew that the feeling of being "no good" was a lie because of where it was leading my heart. I learned a valuable lesson in this experience about discernment and desolation. I know when I feel that way again to be on the alert!*

EXERCISE RECORD

1. When I Awake in the Morning—1 Minute Minimum - 2 Maximum

Location_____ I Exercised Yes____(____Minutes) No____

2. Morning Time Exercise—10 Minutes Minimum -20 Minutes Maximum

Location_____ I Exercised Yes____(____Minutes) No____

3. Examen Exercise Time—15 Minutes Maximum

Location_____ I Exercised Yes____(____Minutes) No____

4. Day Time Exercise—60 Contiguous Minutes (30 or 45 if 60 is not possible)

Location_____ I Exercised Yes____(____Minutes) No____

5. Evening Time Exercise—30 Contiguous Minutes Minimum – 60 Maximum

Location_____ I Exercised Yes____(____Minutes) No____

6. Exercise Journal—1-2 Minutes Once Daily

Location_____ I Exercised Yes____(____Minutes) No____

7. As I Lay Down to Sleep—1 Minute Total

Location_____ I Exercised Yes____(____Minutes) No____

Desolation From the Day – Write no more than two sentences on what decreased your faith, your hope and your love for God and neighbor today.

Consolation From the Day – Write no more than two sentences on what increased your faith, your hope and your love for God and neighbor today.

WEEK 3

DAY SEVEN

Spiritual Exercise for Day or Evening

I will go for a thirty minute walk or run or find a quiet place to sit where I can see nature. I will not listen to music or bring my cell phone with me. I will listen instead to my daydreams, nature, and the people I pass by. I will notice people who appear happy and those who seem to be struggling. I will listen to and watch the world God made for my enjoyment, appreciation and engagement. I realize that I have spiritual energy that reaches to the end of the cosmos and beyond. I will attune my radar to what is holy and reject what is evil. I will listen to what brings me joy or makes me sad.

At the end of your walk, run or quiet time speak to God from your heart and ask God to help you with the one thing you need most today in developing your spiritual radar.

EXERCISE RECORD

1. When I Awake in the Morning—1 Minute Minimum - 2 Maximum

Location_____ I Exercised Yes____(____Minutes) No____

2. Morning Time Exercise—10 Minutes Minimum -20 Minutes Maximum

Location_____ I Exercised Yes____(____Minutes) No____

3. Examen Exercise Time—15 Minutes Maximum

Location_____ I Exercised Yes____(____Minutes) No____

4. Day Time Exercise—60 Contiguous Minutes (30 or 45 if 60 is not possible)

Location_____ I Exercised Yes____(____Minutes) No____

5. Evening Time Exercise—30 Contiguous Minutes Minimum – 60 Maximum

Location_____ I Exercised Yes____(____Minutes) No____

6. Exercise Journal—1-2 Minutes Once Daily

Location_____ I Exercised Yes____(____Minutes) No____

7. As I Lay Down to Sleep—1 Minute Total

Location_____ I Exercised Yes____(____Minutes) No____

8. Night Vigils—30 minutes minimum – 45 maximum

Location_____ I Exercised Yes____(____Minutes) No____

Desolation From the Day – Write no more than two sentences on what decreased your faith, your hope and your love for God and neighbor today.

Consolation From the Day – Write no more than two sentences on what increased your faith, your hope and your love for God and neighbor today.

NOTES

NOTES

Night Vigil

Week 3

DO NOT BE AFRAID!

*Spend thirty to forty-five minutes on this meditation. Be open to all thoughts, feelings, and ideas you have coming from the day. Spend some time talking with God about the things you think significant. Stay here as long as you are comfortable. **Be Alone.***

Icon of the calming of the storm on the Sea of Galilee,
Greek Orthodox Church in Capernaum, Galilee

I. Begin this meditation by asking Jesus to be with you. Ask Jesus to give you the graces he feels will be best for you during this time of the night vigil and this time of Exercise. Specifically ask for the grace to know the good you desire and how you can be tempted to believe that Jesus is not working in you or love you when you feel your weakness and sinfulness. Pray for the grace to know why you can feel bad when God is actually energizing your conscience to know your heart. Use the *Triple Colloquy* below to ask for these graces. Then do the meditation below.

II. Open your Bible to the fifth chapter of Luke, verses one to eleven. Before you read, plan to read it slowly so you can visualize the scenes as they really happened; only place yourself on the boat as one of the disciples. Notice all the details of the people, the smells, the sounds, etc. Keep aware of all the thoughts and feelings you had entering this meditation; only now let yourself be distracted by the events as they unfold before you.

* What is Peter's dilemma? Can you sense what he may be feeling as he speaks to Jesus and asks him to leave him? What is Jesus' response? What does Jesus offer him? Speak to Peter after he is invited by Jesus to be a fisher of people. What is his joy or confusion? What does he say?

III. Pay attention to your reaction to the events that have unfolded before you. See the man leave the presence of Jesus. Walk up to Jesus from your place in the crowd. You are present before Jesus so no one else in the crowd can hear you. Speak to Jesus about what you have just seen and heard. What do you say? What does he say?

IV. Ask Jesus if there is anything in your own life that would prevent you from being a disciple of his. Ask Jesus about any particular things in your own life that cause you shame and make you think Jesus could not or does not love you. What do you say? What is Jesus' response? Stop and listen. What are you thinking and feeling?

V. Pray: *Take, Lord, and receive all my liberty, my memory, my understanding, and my entire will; all that I have and possess. You have given all to me. To you, Lord, I return it. Everything is yours; dispose of it according to your will. Give me only your love and your grace. That is enough for me. Amen!*

TRIPLE COLLOQUY OF SAINT IGNATIUS

First Colloquy, or conversation, will be with Mary. Speak with Mary, using your own words asking her to obtain from her Son the graces described in the first point. When you finish this conversation, pray the *Hail Mary* slowly, thinking of the words and the person to whom you are praying.

Hail Mary, full of grace, The Lord is with thee.
Blessed art thou amongst women
and blessed is the fruit of thy womb, Jesus.
Holy Mary, Mother of God, Pray for us sinners,
now and at the hour of our death.
Amen.

Second Colloquy, or conversation, will be with Jesus. Speak directly to Jesus, asking him to request his Father for the same graces as above. When you finish your conversation, pray the *Anima Christi* slowly, thinking of the words and the person to whom you are praying.

Soul of Christ, sanctify me. Body of Christ, save me.
Blood of Christ, inebriate me. Water from the side of Christ wash me.
Passion of Christ, strengthen me. O Good Jesus, hear me.
Within thy wounds, hide me. Permit me not to be separated from thee.
From the wicked foe, defend me. At the hour of my death, call me,
And bid me come to thee that with thy saints
I may praise thee forever and ever.
Amen.

Third Colloquy, or conversation, will be with God the Father. Ask the Father directly in your own words to give you the graces stated above. When you finish, pray the *Our Father,* thinking of the words and the person to whom you are praying.

Our Father, Who art in heaven, hallowed be thy name.
Thy Kingdom come, Thy will be done, on earth as it is in heaven.
Give us this day our daily bread, and forgive us our trespasses,
As we forgive those who trespass against us.
Lead us not into temptation, but deliver us from evil.
Amen.

WEEK 4

DAY ONE

Spiritual Exercise for Day or Evening

Look Over Your Journal Entries Today
for your Day or Evening Exercise Time

Go over your notes from Week Three Day 6. Pay attention to the phases that describe times in your life when you were "on target" and living in the light of spiritual consolation. Also pay attention to phases that describe times in your life when you were "off target" and living in the shadow of spiritual desolation. See if the two of you can't find a pattern of how you get back on track when off, and off track when on.

There are always patterns to discover and finding them can help us stay more readily on the path toward joy, peace, hope and friendship! Ask yourself about times you were on or off track. How did you manage to get back on the path to life, love, and friendship with God?

EXERCISE RECORD

1. When I Awake in the Morning—1 Minute Minimum - 2 Maximum

Location_____   I Exercised Yes___(___Minutes) No____

2. Morning Time Exercise—10 Minutes Minimum -20 Minutes Maximum

Location_____   I Exercised Yes___(___Minutes) No____

3. Examen Exercise Time—15 Minutes Maximum

Location_____   I Exercised Yes___(___Minutes) No____

4. Day Time Exercise—60 Contiguous Minutes (30 or 45 if 60 is not possible)

Location_____   I Exercised Yes___(___Minutes) No____

5. Evening Time Exercise—30 Contiguous Minutes Minimum – 60 Maximum

Location_____   I Exercised Yes___(___Minutes) No____

6. Exercise Journal—1-2 Minutes Once Daily

Location_____   I Exercised Yes___(___Minutes) No____

7. As I Lay Down to Sleep—1 Minute Total

Location_____   I Exercised Yes___(___Minutes) No____

Desolation From the Day – Write no more than two sentences on what decreased your faith, your hope and your love for God and neighbor today.

Consolation From the Day – Write no more than two sentences on what increased your faith, your hope and your love for God and neighbor today.

WEEK 4

DAY TWO

Read this for your Day or Evening Exercise
and reflect on the questions below.

*RADAR SIGNALS FROM THE DIVINE INSPIRER
OR THE COUNTER-INSPIRER
CAN BOTH MAKE YOU "FEEL GOOD" OR "FEEL BAD"
AND YOU HAVE TO LEARN HOW TO DECODE THEM
BASED ON <u>WHERE</u> THEY GUIDE YOUR HEART*

Counter inspirations, desolations, can make you *feel good* even if they move you away from your authentic human nature—your Heart. *<u>This is a crucially important discernment lesson maybe one of the most important of all!</u>* It is critical in your life-journey that you understand now how inspirations caused by the Divine Inspirer, as well as those inspired by the counter-inspirer, can <u>both *feel good* or *feel bad,*</u> depending on your lifestyle and the corresponding state of your heart and soul.

Keep your eye on the <u>direction</u> the inspirations lead, (away from authenticity—your false heart) or towards authenticity (your true heart). This is a kind of leadership discernment in which the "feelings" themselves are not as important as the direction the feelings "inspire" you towards. As a spiritual person, you will need to care as much or more about the *life-direction of your heart* than whether something makes you *feel good* or *feel bad* in the moment.

Reflection Question:

Pray to the Divine-Inspirer to have your memory "energized." Ask for the grace to think of a "lifestyle choice" the Scriptures, the Tradition and the Catholic Church considers inauthentic but that you have decided is authentic. Think. What is that lifestyle that comes to mind where you find yourself in disagreement?

Example: "I think it is important for me to make up my own mind on what is right and wrong and not allow the Church to tell me how to live my life. I feel good about being in command of my own decisions and feel discouraged when someone else tells me how to live my life or what I can and can't do.

From the discernment lesson above, based on how confusing "feelings" of right and wrong can be based on the "direction" a lifestyle leads, should this person be challenged to rethink their position?

Briefly write your about the lifestyle choice you considered and if you have any new thoughts based on this key spiritual discernment guideline.

EXERCISE RECORD

1. When I Awake in the Morning—1 Minute Minimum - 2 Maximum

Location_____ I Exercised Yes___ (___Minutes) No____

2. Morning Time Exercise—10 Minutes Minimum -20 Minutes Maximum

Location_____ I Exercised Yes___ (___Minutes) No____

3. Examen Exercise Time—15 Minutes Maximum

Location_____ I Exercised Yes___ (___Minutes) No____

4. Day Time Exercise—60 Contiguous Minutes (30 or 45 if 60 is not possible)

Location_____ I Exercised Yes___ (___Minutes) No____

5. Evening Time Exercise—30 Contiguous Minutes Minimum – 60 Maximum

Location_____ I Exercised Yes___ (___Minutes) No____

6. Exercise Journal—1-2 Minutes Once Daily

Location_____ I Exercised Yes___ (___Minutes) No____

7. As I Lay Down to Sleep—1 Minute Total

Location_____ I Exercised Yes___ (___Minutes) No____

Desolation From the Day – Write no more than two sentences on what decreased your faith, your hope and your love for God and neighbor today.

Consolation From the Day – Write no more than two sentences on what increased your faith, your hope and your love for God and neighbor today.

WEEK 4

DAY THREE

Spiritual Exercise for Day or Evening

I will go to Daily Mass alone or with a friend during my Day or Evening Exercise Time. Today, I will offer the Mass for the needs of my family and friends.

EXERCISE RECORD

1. When I Awake in the Morning—1 Minute Minimum - 2 Maximum

Location_____ I Exercised Yes___(___Minutes) No___

2. Morning Time Exercise—10 Minutes Minimum -20 Minutes Maximum

Location_____ I Exercised Yes___(___Minutes) No___

3. Examen Exercise Time—15 Minutes Maximum

Location_____ I Exercised Yes___(___Minutes) No___

4. Day Time Exercise—60 Contiguous Minutes (30 or 45 if 60 is not possible)

Location_____ I Exercised Yes___(___Minutes) No___

5. Evening Time Exercise—30 Contiguous Minutes Minimum – 60 Maximum

Location_____ I Exercised Yes___(___Minutes) No___

6. Exercise Journal—1-2 Minutes Once Daily

Location_____ I Exercised Yes___(___Minutes) No___

7. As I Lay Down to Sleep—1 Minute Total

Location_____ I Exercised Yes___(___Minutes) No___

Desolation From the Day – Write no more than two sentences on what decreased your faith, your hope and your love for God and neighbor today.

Consolation From the Day – Write no more than two sentences on what increased your faith, your hope and your love for God and neighbor today.

Week 4

Day Four

Read this for your Day or Evening Exercise
and reflect on the questions below.

SPIRITUAL RADAR SIGNALS
WHEN FOLLOWED IN ONE DIRECTION OR ANOTHER
CREATE ENERGY FIELDS OR "LIFESYTLES"
THAT REVEAL WHICH "INSPIRER' YOU ARE FOLLOWING

Remember there really is a Divine-Inspirer who is Lord of the Universe and a counter-inspirer who is the dark lord and the enemy of human nature. These are the real forces that are guiding hearts towards life or death. For this Exercise we focus more sharply on identifying the ways in which these spiritual states manifest in our culture today as lifestyles. Throughout your life today, continue to pay attention to your affective moods to *feel* the states of consolation and desolation in your heart. Look for lifestyle attitudes or choices that bear the signature characteristics of consolation and desolation.

Individuals and groups can consciously or unconsciously live either aligned with life and joy—be a true heart aligned with Gospel values and an authentic self *or* death and sadness—a false heart not aligned with

Gospel values. The book of Deuteronomy powerfully captures this reality. God placed before the people Israel two distinct choices:

I call heaven and earth today to witness against you: I have set before you life and death, the blessing and the curse. Choose life, then, that you and your descendants may live, by loving the LORD, your God, obeying his voice, and holding fast to him. For that will mean life for you, a long life for you to live on the land which the LORD swore to your ancestors, to Abraham, Isaac, and Jacob, to give to them (Dt. 30: 18-20).

> Remember the key lesson from our previous Exercise: things that feel bad can move us towards life and things that feel good can move us towards death.
>
> We have to look not at what makes us feel good or feel bad, but the lifestyles and life-direction feelings move us towards.

If we have become insensitive to God's presence, our hearts can be moving away from the Author of life. We may not be aware of this because of a silenced conscience.

If you live in a culture or a sub-culture that is also insensitive to the Author of Life, you can be doubly challenged to find the path back to life---to your truest self.

When you are sensitive to the Author of life, your *heart* is moving in the direction of producing fruit that endures to eternity. This will be correct even if you live in a culture that is insensitive to life's Author.

Christ promises: *Blessed are you when they insult you and persecute you and utter every kind of evil against you [falsely] because of me. Rejoice and be glad, for your reward will be great in heaven. Thus they persecuted the prophets who were before you (Mt 5: 11-12).*

Reflection Question

Pray to the Divine-Inspirer to have your memory "energized." Think of a group you privately supported whose lifestyle was "Gospel inspired" but it was not popular with the majority of your peers. Perhaps the lifestyle was linked to some hot-button social or moral issue like the environment, sex or marriage, immigration, the economy or politics.

What was the "lifestyle" that made them unpopular? Did you make your support known or keep quiet about it because of fear or majority group pressure?

Write briefly in your journal about one such experience: why did you support the group and how did you act?

EXERCISE RECORD

1. When I Awake in the Morning—1 Minute Minimum - 2 Maximum

Location_____   I Exercised Yes___(___Minutes) No___

2. Morning Time Exercise—10 Minutes Minimum -20 Minutes Maximum

Location_____   I Exercised Yes___(___Minutes) No___

3. Examen Exercise Time—15 Minutes Maximum

Location_____   I Exercised Yes___(___Minutes) No___

4. Day Time Exercise—60 Contiguous Minutes (30 or 45 if 60 is not possible)

Location_____   I Exercised Yes___(___Minutes) No___

5. Evening Time Exercise—30 Contiguous Minutes Minimum – 60 Maximum

Location_____   I Exercised Yes___(___Minutes) No___

6. Exercise Journal—1-2 Minutes Once Daily

Location_____   I Exercised Yes___(___Minutes) No___

7. As I Lay Down to Sleep—1 Minute Total

Location_____   I Exercised Yes___(___Minutes) No___

Desolation From the Day – Write no more than two sentences on what decreased your faith, your hope and your love for God and neighbor today.

Consolation From the Day – Write no more than two sentences on what increased your faith, your hope and your love for God and neighbor today.

Week 4

Day Five

Spiritual Exercise for Day or Evening

I will go for a thirty minute walk or run or find a quiet place to sit where I can see nature. I will not listen to music or bring my cell phone with me. I will listen instead to my daydreams, nature, and the people who pass by. I will notice people who appear happy and those who seem to be struggling. I will listen to and watch the world God made for my enjoyment, appreciation and engagement. I realize that I have spiritual energy that reaches to the end of the cosmos and beyond. I will attune my radar to what is holy and reject what is evil. I will listen to what brings me joy or makes me sad.

At the end of your walk, run or quiet time speak to God from your heart and ask God to help you distinguishing between good and bad feelings that are the opposite of what they appear to reveal: how things that feel bad might be pointing in a good direction and how things that feel good, might be pointing in a bad direction.

EXERCISE RECORD

1. When I Awake in the Morning—1 Minute Minimum - 2 Maximum

Location_____   I Exercised Yes___(___Minutes) No___

2. Morning Time Exercise—10 Minutes Minimum -20 Minutes Maximum

Location_____   I Exercised Yes___(___Minutes) No___

3. Examen Exercise Time—15 Minutes Maximum

Location_____   I Exercised Yes___(___Minutes) No___

4. Day Time Exercise—60 Contiguous Minutes (30 or 45 if 60 is not possible)

Location_____   I Exercised Yes___(___Minutes) No___

5. Evening Time Exercise—30 Contiguous Minutes Minimum – 60 Maximum

Location_____   I Exercised Yes___(___Minutes) No___

6. Exercise Journal—1-2 Minutes Once Daily

Location_____   I Exercised Yes___(___Minutes) No___

7. As I Lay Down to Sleep—1 Minute Total

Location_____   I Exercised Yes___(___Minutes) No___

Desolation From the Day – Write no more than two sentences on what decreased your faith, your hope and your love for God and neighbor today.

Consolation From the Day – Write no more than two sentences on what increased your faith, your hope and your love for God and neighbor today.

WEEK 4

DAY SIX

Spiritual Exercise for Day or Evening

Read this for your Day or Evening Exercise
and reflect on the questions below.

SPIRITUAL RADAR SIGNALS
LEAD TO LIFESTYLES AND SUBCULTURES

We can choose to align ourselves with sub-cultures that are counter to the life proposed by the Commandments, Scripture and the teaching Church—the life proposed by the very embodiment of human nature, Jesus Christ. It is difficult to be objective about anti-Gospel or "anti-Christ" lifestyles when we are immersed in these sub-cultures or peer groups.

For example, youth who get involved with a group of peers that is using or abusing illegal or performance-enhancing drugs, it "get sucked in" and once they are sucked in, it is hard to fully see the damage it is doing to them.   That is why we call it a "drug culture." We can embed ourselves in these groups and allow definitions of happiness, success, the good, the beautiful, and the moral to isolate us from the data coming from deep in our divinely inspired heat.

These anti-Gospel sub-cultures can be economic, political, artistic, ethnic, intellectual, sexual, athletic, addiction-based, and Web-based or just about anything else that a group endorses. The main challenge is that we can embed ourselves in these cultures, allowing their definitions of happiness, success, the good, the beautiful, and the moral to isolate us from the data coming from deep in our divinely inspired heart. Do you see this happening in your friendship groups?

So, *consolation* and *desolation* can be described comprehensively as *lifestyles.* By thinking about them that way, we can measure the arc of our lives against the traditional categories of goodness the Church has defined.

Reflection Questions

Pray to the Divine-Inspirer to have your memory "energized." Think of one lifestyle the "majority" defends and one lifestyle the "majority" denounces. Examine each lifestyle in light of whether it aligns or not with the Gospel, Jesus and the Church. Why do you think one is defended and the other denounced?

Example: Pope Francis denounced gender ideologies saying that there was a war against marriage. He was both praised and ridiculed in the media for this position. He also called for every migrant who needed safety to be allowed in the countries of Europe. He was also praised and ridiculed for this position.

In light of what you have learned about spiritual discernment, write very brief observations in your journal about each instance of the rightness or wrongness of what is defended or denounced and what you have come to believe at this point in your spiritual journey.

EXERCISE RECORD

1. When I Awake in the Morning—1 Minute Minimum - 2 Maximum

Location_____   I Exercised Yes____(____Minutes) No____

2. Morning Time Exercise—10 Minutes Minimum -20 Minutes Maximum

Location_____   I Exercised Yes____(____Minutes) No____

3. Examen Exercise Time—15 Minutes Maximum

Location_____   I Exercised Yes____(____Minutes) No____

4. Day Time Exercise—60 Contiguous Minutes (30 or 45 if 60 is not possible)

Location_____   I Exercised Yes____(____Minutes) No____

5. Evening Time Exercise—30 Contiguous Minutes Minimum – 60 Maximum

Location_____   I Exercised Yes____(____Minutes) No____

6. Exercise Journal—1-2 Minutes Once Daily

Location_____   I Exercised Yes____(____Minutes) No____

7. As I Lay Down to Sleep—1 Minute Total

Location_____   I Exercised Yes____(____Minutes) No____

Desolation From the Day – Write no more than two sentences on what decreased your faith, your hope and your love for God and neighbor today.

Consolation From the Day – Write no more than two sentences on what increased your faith, your hope and your love for God and neighbor today.

WEEK 4

DAY SEVEN

Spiritual Exercise for Day or Evening

Take some time today to reflect on your journal entries on consolation and desolation as lifestyles. If you need prompting on what to look for below are some ideas you can pursue. You may choose to do this with your Mass companion.

What lifestyles do you engage in that you now realize are *spiritual consolation*?

Are you in lifestyles that you realize now are *spiritual desolation?*

How have you been courageous or fearful in defending what you think is right or wrong with your friends and family?

Here's how I think I've been courageous...(give an example)

Here's how I think I've been too scared to speak up....(give an example).

EXERCISE RECORD

1. When I Awake in the Morning—1 Minute Minimum - 2 Maximum

Location_____ I Exercised Yes____(____Minutes) No____

2. Morning Time Exercise—10 Minutes Minimum -20 Minutes Maximum

Location_____ I Exercised Yes____(____Minutes) No____

3. Examen Exercise Time—15 Minutes Maximum

Location_____ I Exercised Yes____(____Minutes) No____

4. Day Time Exercise—60 Contiguous Minutes (30 or 45 if 60 is not possible)

Location_____ I Exercised Yes____(____Minutes) No____

5. Evening Time Exercise—30 Contiguous Minutes Minimum – 60 Maximum

Location_____ I Exercised Yes____(____Minutes) No____

6. Exercise Journal—1-2 Minutes Once Daily

Location_____ I Exercised Yes____(____Minutes) No____

7. As I Lay Down to Sleep—1 Minute Total

Location_____ I Exercised Yes____(____Minutes) No____

8. Night Vigils—30 minutes minimum – 45 maximum

Location_____ I Exercised Yes____(____Minutes) No____

Desolation From the Day – _Write no more than two sentences_ on what decreased your faith, your hope and your love for God and neighbor today.

Consolation From the Day – _Write no more than two sentences_ on what increased your faith, your hope and your love for God and neighbor today.

NOTES

NOTES

NIGHT VIGIL

WEEK 4

JESUS ACCUSED OF BEING THE DEVIL

Spend thirty to forty-five minutes on this meditation. Be open to all thoughts, feelings, and ideas you have coming from the day. Spend some time talking with God about the things you think significant. Stay here as long as you are comfortable. **Be Alone.**

Artist Unknown

I. Begin this meditation by asking Jesus to be with you. Ask Jesus to give you the graces he feels will be best for you during this time of the night vigil and this time of Exercise. Specifically ask for the grace to know how the religious leaders of Jesus' day could have mistaken him and his message as satanic. Pray to understand how the values of Jesus can be seen as evil and hateful in our own time. Use the *Triple Colloquy* below to ask for these graces and do this first. Then spend the rest of your time with the meditation below.

II. Open your Bible to the twelfth chapter of Matthew, verses twenty-two to thirty-two. Before you read, plan to read it slowly so you can visualize the scenes as they really happened; only place yourself in the scene to see and feel the profound tensions between Jesus and the religious leaders. Notice all the details of the people, the smells, the sounds, etc. Keep aware of all the thoughts and feelings you had entering this meditation; only now let yourself be distracted by the events as they unfold before you.

* Watch Jesus perform his act of curing the possessed man, restoring his sight and hearing. How does the crowd react? How does the man cured thank Jesus? Why are the religious leaders so angered by Jesus' act of mercy? What are the tensions you feel in the crowd between Jesus, his followers and those denouncing him? How do the leaders react when Jesus speaks to them about blasphemy against the Holy Spirit?

III. Pay attention to your reaction to the events that have unfolded before you. See the man leave the presence of Jesus. Walk up to Jesus from your place in the crowd. You are present before Jesus so no one else in the crowd can hear you. Speak to Jesus about what you have just seen and heard. What do you say? What does he say? What invitation does he extend to you?

IV. Ask Jesus if there is anything you have confused as evil or hateful that is actually holy and good. Tell him why you are confused. What does he tell you? What do you say in return? What is Jesus' response? Stop and listen. What are you thinking and feeling?

V. Pray: *Take, Lord, and receive all my liberty, my memory, my understanding, and my entire will; all that I have and possess. You have given all to me. To you, Lord, I return it. Everything is yours; dispose of it according to your will. Give me only your love and your grace. That is enough for me. Amen!*

TRIPLE COLLOQUY OF SAINT IGNATIUS

First Colloquy, or conversation, will be with Mary. Speak with Mary, using your own words asking her to obtain from her Son the graces described in point one above. When you finish this conversation, pray the *Hail Mary* slowly, thinking of the words and the person to whom you are praying.

Hail Mary, full of grace, The Lord is with thee.
Blessed art thou amongst women
and blessed is the fruit of thy womb, Jesus.
Holy Mary, Mother of God, Pray for us sinners,
now and at the hour of our death.
Amen.

Second Colloquy, or conversation, will be with Jesus. Speak directly to Jesus, asking him to request his Father for the same graces as above. When you finish your conversation, pray the *Anima Christi* slowly, thinking of the words and the person to whom you are praying.

Soul of Christ, sanctify me. Body of Christ, save me.
Blood of Christ, inebriate me. Water from the side of Christ wash me.
Passion of Christ, strengthen me. O Good Jesus, hear me. Within thy
wounds, hide me. Permit me not to be separated from thee. From the
wicked foe, defend me. At the hour of my death, call me, and bid me
come to thee that with thy saints I may praise thee forever and ever.
Amen.

Third Colloquy, or conversation, will be with God the Father. Ask the Father directly in your own words to give you the graces stated above. When you finish, pray the *Our Father*, thinking of the words and the person to whom you are praying.

Our Father, Who art in heaven, hallowed be thy name.
Thy Kingdom come, Thy will be done, on earth as it is in heaven. Give us
this day our daily bread, and forgive us our trespasses, As we forgive
those who trespass against us.
Lead us not into temptation, but deliver us from evil.
Amen!

WEEK 5

DAY ONE

Spiritual Exercise for Day or Evening

I will go for a thirty minute walk or run or find a quiet place to sit where I can see nature. I will not listen to music or bring my cell phone with me. I will listen instead to my daydreams, nature and the people who pass by. I will notice people who appear happy and those who seem to be struggling. I will listen to and watch the world God made for my enjoyment, appreciation and engagement. I realize that I have spiritual energy that reaches to the end of the cosmos and beyond. I will attune my radar to what is holy and reject what is evil. I will listen to what brings me joy or makes me sad.

At the end of your walk, run or quiet time speak to God from your heart and ask God to help you with the one thing you need most today in understanding how both good and evil work in your life story.

EXERCISE RECORD

1. When I Awake in the Morning—1 Minute Minimum - 2 Maximum

Location_____ I Exercised Yes____(___Minutes) No____

2. Morning Time Exercise—10 Minutes Minimum -20 Minutes Maximum

Location_____ I Exercised Yes____(___Minutes) No____

3. Examen Exercise Time—15 Minutes Maximum

Location_____ I Exercised Yes____(___Minutes) No____

4. Day Time Exercise—60 Contiguous Minutes (30 or 45 if 60 is not possible)

Location_____ I Exercised Yes____(___Minutes) No____

5. Evening Time Exercise—30 Contiguous Minutes Minimum – 60 Maximum

Location_____ I Exercised Yes____(___Minutes) No____

6. Exercise Journal—1-2 Minutes Once Daily

Location_____ I Exercised Yes____(___Minutes) No____

7. As I Lay Down to Sleep—1 Minute Total

Location_____ I Exercised Yes____(___Minutes) No____

Desolation From the Day – Write no more than two sentences on what decreased your faith, your hope and your love for God and neighbor today.

Consolation From the Day – Write no more than two sentences on what increased your faith, your hope and your love for God and neighbor today.

Week 5

Day Two

Spiritual Exercise for Day or Evening

Read this for your Day or Evening Exercise
and reflect on the questions below.

DIVINE-INSPIRATION AS A LIFESTYLE

*WHEN FOLLOWED TO THE LIGHT, SPIRITUAL RADAR SIGNALS CREATE AN
ENERGY FIELD OR "LIFESYTLE" WITH WAVES THAT IGNITE YOUR HEART
TO POSITIVELY ALTER THE UNIVERSE*

Both the Divine-Inspirer and the counter-inspirer we have learned, are
seeking to define our lifestyle—our life! Jesus wants us to follow him as
Way, Truth, and the Life.

When you are *evolving* under the Divine inspirations aligned to
thoughts, words and deeds your lifestyle will be harmonious with the
Scripture, Commandments and the teaching Church. While you are
following this lifestyle, you will be more filled with faith, hope and
love—you will be more humble and selfless—most fully yourself. When
you live this way you positively influence all those who come in your
path.

This happens because you are on the wavelength of Jesus, the Holy Spirit and the Father whose Love guides the course of creation and all ambassadors of light—all people who are true to their hearts.

When you are following the radar signals of the Divine-Inspirer, the Divine author of your human nature will provide "heart-verification" that you'll experience as the awakening of your power of reason and the stirring of your conscience.

Reflection Questions:

Pray to the Divine-Inspirer to have your memory "energized."

Can you remember ever making a deliberate and conscious choice to align your lifestyle and heart to the values of the Gospel and Jesus? If yes, when was it and what was the context?

Example: *The Gospel tells us to turn the other cheek. This was very hard for me when I was humiliated by a hurtful comment at work. Yet I realized the person who said this hurtful thing was also hurting. Although sorely tempted, I did not want this incident to escalate into a fight. I just told the person I hoped somebody does something nice for you today and I walked away to keep a "peaceful" lifestyle.*

Can you remember a time when you veered slightly off course but the "radar" alerted you to stay on course? If yes, what was the context?

Write very brief reflections in your journal.

EXERCISE RECORD

1. When I Awake in the Morning—1 Minute Minimum - 2 Maximum

Location_____   I Exercised Yes___(___Minutes) No___

2. Morning Time Exercise—10 Minutes Minimum -20 Minutes Maximum

Location_____   I Exercised Yes___(___Minutes) No___

3. Examen Exercise Time—15 Minutes Maximum

Location_____   I Exercised Yes___(___Minutes) No___

4. Day Time Exercise—60 Contiguous Minutes (30 or 45 if 60 is not possible)

Location_____   I Exercised Yes___(___Minutes) No___

5. Evening Time Exercise—30 Contiguous Minutes Minimum – 60 Maximum

Location_____   I Exercised Yes___(___Minutes) No___

6. Exercise Journal—1-2 Minutes Once Daily

Location_____   I Exercised Yes___(___Minutes) No___

7. As I Lay Down to Sleep—1 Minute Total

Location_____   I Exercised Yes___(___Minutes) No___

Desolation From the Day – Write no more than two sentences on what decreased your faith, your hope and your love for God and neighbor today.

Consolation From the Day – Write no more than two sentences on what increased your faith, your hope and your love for God and neighbor today.

Week 5

Day Three

Spiritual Exercise for Day or Evening

I will go to Daily Mass alone or with a friend during my Day or Evening Exercise Time. Offer your Mass today that everyone in your family can always choose lifestyles that build up faith, hope and love.

EXERCISE RECORD

1. When I Awake in the Morning—1 Minute Minimum - 2 Maximum

Location_____ I Exercised Yes___(___Minutes) No___

2. Morning Time Exercise—10 Minutes Minimum -20 Minutes Maximum

Location_____ I Exercised Yes___(___Minutes) No___

3. Examen Exercise Time—15 Minutes Maximum

Location_____ I Exercised Yes___(___Minutes) No___

4. Day Time Exercise—60 Contiguous Minutes (30 or 45 if 60 is not possible)

Location_____ I Exercised Yes___(___Minutes) No___

5. Evening Time Exercise—30 Contiguous Minutes Minimum – 60 Maximum

Location_____ I Exercised Yes___(___Minutes) No___

6. Exercise Journal—1-2 Minutes Once Daily

Location_____ I Exercised Yes___(___Minutes) No___

7. As I Lay Down to Sleep—1 Minute Total

Location_____ I Exercised Yes___(___Minutes) No___

Desolation From the Day – Write no more than two sentences on what decreased your faith, your hope and your love for God and neighbor today.

Consolation From the Day – Write no more than two sentences on what increased your faith, your hope and your love for God and neighbor today.

Week 5

Day Four

Spiritual Exercise for Day or Evening

Read this for your Day or Evening Exercise
and reflect on the questions below.

COUNTER-INSPIRATION AS A LIFESTYLE

*WHEN FOLLOWED AWAY FROM THE LIGHT, SPIRITUAL RADAR SIGNALS
CREATE AN ENERGY FIELD OR "LIFESYTLE" WITH WAVES THAT DISTORT
YOUR HEART TO NEGATIVELY ALTER THE UNIVERSE.*

Are you *evolving* under the counter inspirations opposed to true love?
Are your thoughts, words and deeds opposed to the Commandments,
Scripture and the teaching Church?

The enemy of your human nature is able to hold you in the grip of false
loves by deceit and false appearances. How? What leads you away from
God, from Love, appears pleasurable, and is presented as good, morally
right, life-giving, fashionable, and enlightened. The false loves are like a
drug for the interior pain we feel.

.

Reflection Exercise:

Pray to the Divine-Inspirer to have your memory "energized."

> *This is an important discernment lesson.* Think of Divine inspiration (spiritual consolation) as a healthy lifestyle that may not feel healthy because *it is not* supported by the culture or sub-cultures or the peer groups in which you live.
>
> Think of counter inspiration (spiritual desolation) as an unhealthy lifestyle that might not feel unhealthy because *it is* supported by the culture or sub-cultures or the peer groups in which you live.

Map some of the influences in your life using the small chart below of two sub-cultures or peer groups where you spend most of your time each week: home culture, work environments, Internet, social groups and associations, exercise or athletic environments, groups aligned with arts and or entertainment, political parties, and the cultures of film, television and or gaming where you spend time.

Next to the two sub-cultures, write one sentence about what you believe is its *signature characteristic* regarding its *overall* influence on your lifestyle. Does it lead to God and your faith or away?

If it leads away, write one sentence about how you could leave it or minimize its negative impact on you.

Sub-Culture or Peer Group	Its Signature Characteristics

EXERCISE RECORD

1. When I Awake in the Morning—1 Minute Minimum - 2 Maximum

Location_____ I Exercised Yes___(___Minutes) No____

2. Morning Time Exercise—10 Minutes Minimum -20 Minutes Maximum

Location_____ I Exercised Yes___(___Minutes) No____

3. Examen Exercise Time—15 Minutes Maximum

Location_____ I Exercised Yes___(___Minutes) No____

4. Day Time Exercise—60 Contiguous Minutes (30 or 45 if 60 is not possible)

Location_____ I Exercised Yes___(___Minutes) No____

5. Evening Time Exercise—30 Contiguous Minutes Minimum – 60 Maximum

Location_____ I Exercised Yes___(___Minutes) No____

6. Exercise Journal—1-2 Minutes Once Daily

Location_____ I Exercised Yes___(___Minutes) No____

7. As I Lay Down to Sleep—1 Minute Total

Location_____ I Exercised Yes___(___Minutes) No____

Desolation From the Day – Write no more than two sentences on what decreased your faith, your hope and your love for God and neighbor today.

Consolation From the Day – Write no more than two sentences on what increased your faith, your hope and your love for God and neighbor today.

Week 5

Day Five

I will go for a thirty minute walk or run or find a quiet place to sit where I can see nature. I will not listen to music or bring my cell phone with me. I will listen instead to my daydreams, nature and the people who pass by. I will notice people who appear happy and those who seem to be struggling. I will listen to and watch the world God made for my enjoyment, appreciation and engagement. I realize that I have spiritual energy that reaches to the end of the cosmos and beyond. I will attune my radar to what is holy and reject what is evil. I will listen to what brings me joy or makes me sad.

At the end of your walk, run or quiet time speak to God from your heart and ask God to help you with the one thing you need most today to develop a consistent lifestyle that is aligned with the Gospel of Jesus Christ.

EXERCISE RECORD

1. When I Awake in the Morning—1 Minute Minimum - 2 Maximum

Location_____ I Exercised Yes____(____Minutes) No____

2. Morning Time Exercise—10 Minutes Minimum -20 Minutes Maximum

Location_____ I Exercised Yes____(____Minutes) No____

3. Examen Exercise Time—15 Minutes Maximum

Location_____ I Exercised Yes____(____Minutes) No____

4. Day Time Exercise—60 Contiguous Minutes (30 or 45 if 60 is not possible)

Location_____ I Exercised Yes____(____Minutes) No____

5. Evening Time Exercise—30 Contiguous Minutes Minimum – 60 Maximum

Location_____ I Exercised Yes____(____Minutes) No____

6. Exercise Journal—1-2 Minutes Once Daily

Location_____ I Exercised Yes____(____Minutes) No____

7. As I Lay Down to Sleep—1 Minute Total

Location_____ I Exercised Yes____(____Minutes) No____

Desolation From the Day – Write no more than two sentences on what decreased your faith, your hope and your love for God and neighbor today.

Consolation From the Day – Write no more than two sentences on what increased your faith, your hope and your love for God and neighbor today.

WEEK 5

DAY SIX

Spiritual Exercise for Day or Evening

Read this for your Day or Evening Exercise and
reflect on the questions below.

*HOW TO RESPOND WHEN SIGNALS FROM THE DARKNESS
TRICK YOU TO TURN FROM THE LIGHT*

Diffusing Counter Inspirations:

Ignatius offers four principles for how we ought to act when tempted by
the counter inspirations of desolation. Here are the first two:

1)   *When we are spiritually desolate--experiencing a loss of faith,
hope and love--we should **NEVER change course** away from the positive
resolutions and decisions we reached while previously under the
influence of the Divine inspiration of consolation. This means: A heart*
must be vigilant when tempted by an urgent or compelling impulse *to
act immediately.*

If you are in an emergency situation, of course, you must act quickly,
but Ignatius is talking here about the feeling of anxious urgency to reach

a decision or engage an action that really needs more patience. For instance, you might know in your heart that you should wait another week to make a decision about something hugely important to you but you just impulsively decide. This may end up being a course change that you regret later.

2)   *During times of desolation, redouble efforts to open and orient your heart to God. Use prayer, examination of conscience, and perhaps some simple penance or fasting to seek God's grace, patience, and peace (Mk 9:29).*

Reflection Exercise:

Pray to the Divine-Inspirer to have your memory "energized." Remember a time when you were on a peaceful good course but then counter-inspirations upset you. The upset compelled you to make a hasty decision and looking back you can see you acted on fear, not peace. What was the context? Remember the anxiety you felt.

Now remember a time when you were upset and turned to prayer and your spiritual disciplines for help and you found peace and calm. What was the context? Remember the relief you felt.

Briefly write these memories in your journal.

Counter inspirations make it difficult to *see and feel* authentic human nature—your true heart. Increasing positive efforts on spiritual fronts might feel incredibly difficult.

Yet St. Ignatius' experience demonstrated that we need at these times *extra exercise* of spirit and body to resist desolation. A determined spirit is necessary during such times.

Also, be attentive to thoughts, words, or deeds that are based on *inaccurate* assessments of your authentic human nature. Allow the times of desolation to instruct you!

EXERCISE RECORD

1. When I Awake in the Morning—1 Minute Minimum - 2 Maximum

Location_____ I Exercised Yes____(____Minutes) No____

2. Morning Time Exercise—10 Minutes Minimum -20 Minutes Maximum

Location_____ I Exercised Yes____(____Minutes) No____

3. Examen Exercise Time—15 Minutes Maximum

Location_____ I Exercised Yes____(____Minutes) No____

4. Day Time Exercise—60 Contiguous Minutes (30 or 45 if 60 is not possible)

Location_____ I Exercised Yes____(____Minutes) No____

5. Evening Time Exercise—30 Contiguous Minutes Minimum – 60 Maximum

Location_____ I Exercised Yes____(____Minutes) No____

6. Exercise Journal—1-2 Minutes Once Daily

Location_____ I Exercised Yes____(____Minutes) No____

7. As I Lay Down to Sleep—1 Minute Total

Location_____ I Exercised Yes____(____Minutes) No____

Desolation From the Day – Write no more than two sentences on what decreased your faith, your hope and your love for God and neighbor today.

Consolation From the Day – Write no more than two sentences on what increased your faith, your hope and your love for God and neighbor today.

Week 5

Day Seven

Spiritual Exercise for Day or Evening

I will go to Daily Mass alone or with a friend during my Day or Evening Exercise Time. Offer your Mass today in gratitude for the best insight you have received so far on this spiritual journey.

EXERCISE RECORD

1. When I Awake in the Morning—1 Minute Minimum - 2 Maximum

Location_____ I Exercised Yes____(____Minutes) No____

2. Morning Time Exercise—10 Minutes Minimum -20 Minutes Maximum

Location_____ I Exercised Yes____(____Minutes) No____

3. Examen Exercise Time—15 Minutes Maximum

Location_____ I Exercised Yes____(____Minutes) No____

4. Day Time Exercise—60 Contiguous Minutes (30 or 45 if 60 is not possible)

Location_____ I Exercised Yes____(____Minutes) No____

5. Evening Time Exercise—30 Contiguous Minutes Minimum – 60 Maximum

Location_____ I Exercised Yes____(____Minutes) No____

6. Exercise Journal—1-2 Minutes Once Daily

Location_____ I Exercised Yes____(____Minutes) No____

7. As I Lay Down to Sleep—1 Minute Total

Location_____ I Exercised Yes____(____Minutes) No____

8. Night Vigils—30 minutes minimum – 45 maximum

Location_____ I Exercised Yes____(____Minutes) No____

Desolation From the Day – Write no more than two sentences on what decreased your faith, your hope and your love for God and neighbor today.

Consolation From the Day – Write no more than two sentences on what increased your faith, your hope and your love for God and neighbor today.

NOTES

NOTES

NIGHT VIGIL
WEEK 5

<u>*THE LOST SON AND THE DUTIFUL SON*</u>

The Prodigal Son

Rembrant

Spend thirty to forty-five minutes on this meditation. Do only one section at a time and do not read ahead. Do not feel compelled to finish the whole sheet. St ay with each section until your heart suggests moving on. Do not read or write after this meditation except perhaps a short journal entry. **Be Alone.**

I. Gather in what your senses are experiencing. Breathe in the Spirit of God. Breathe out whatever is troubling, distracting, or burdensome. Be aware of all the thoughts and feelings coming from the day so far.

II. Talk to Jesus in your own words about your desire for this particular grace: that I may come to know lifestyles that give life and those that do not. Ask Jesus for a discerning heart that you may choose the path of life and always turn away from the path of death.. Stay with this for as long as you like. Don't feel compelled to move on unless your heart suggests.

III. We read in the story of the lost son and the dutiful son that both the life of self-indulgence and the life of dutiful obedience are wrong. Both the son who "broke" all the Commandments and the one, who "dutifully" followed them all, were both lost. Lifestyles that have the appearance of goodness can be as death-dealing as those that openly violate Gospel values. In Luke chapter fifteen, verses eleven to thirty-two, read the very familiar Gospel story of these two sons and the father who loves them. Visualize their lives as you read the story and see the emptiness from which they both suffered.

As you watch their lives, see if you have in your own life any of the temptations of the lost or the dutiful son. Listen to their lives and your own. Most especially, feel the embrace of the Father who loves you and will always welcome you home—even when you have strayed from his house.

Then watch the crowd as Jesus tells the story. Who in the crowd do you see living a life of self-indulgence and who a life of legalistic duty? See and experience the events as they happen. Notice everything about what is happening to Jesus and yourself. Do not move to the next section unless your heart suggests.

Pray with Luke 15: 11-32

IV. ASK THE LORD FOR HIS HELP in letting go of what binds you; of what keeps you from freely coming home if you have strayed, or from accepting with joy those who have been lost but found by the Father's Mercy. Pray that Jesus make you true to your heart's deepest desires.

V. Following the meditation, bring your own prayer period to a close by slowly praying the *Our Father,* listening to the words in your heart as you pray.

Week 6

Day One

Spiritual Exercise for Day or Evening

I will go for a thirty minute walk or run or find a quiet place to sit where I can see nature. I will not listen to music or bring my cell phone with me. I will listen instead to my daydreams, nature and the people who pass by. I will notice people who appear happy and those who seem to be struggling. I will listen to and watch the world God made for my enjoyment, appreciation and engagement. I realize that I have spiritual energy that reaches to the end of the cosmos and beyond. I will attune my radar to what is holy and reject what is evil. I will listen to what brings me joy or makes me sad.

At the end of your walk, run or quiet time speak to God from your heart and ask God to help you with the one thing you need most today in always trusting God will lead you to what is right if you ask for the Holy Spirit's help.

EXERCISE RECORD

1. When I Awake in the Morning—1 Minute Minimum - 2 Maximum

Location_____   I Exercised Yes___(___Minutes) No___

2. Morning Time Exercise—10 Minutes Minimum -20 Minutes Maximum

Location_____   I Exercised Yes___(___Minutes) No___

3. Examen Exercise Time—15 Minutes Maximum

Location_____   I Exercised Yes___(___Minutes) No___

4. Day Time Exercise—60 Contiguous Minutes (30 or 45 if 60 is not possible)

Location_____   I Exercised Yes___(___Minutes) No___

5. Evening Time Exercise—30 Contiguous Minutes Minimum – 60 Maximum

Location_____   I Exercised Yes___(___Minutes) No___

6. Exercise Journal—1-2 Minutes Once Daily

Location_____   I Exercised Yes___(___Minutes) No___

7. As I Lay Down to Sleep—1 Minute Total

Location_____   I Exercised Yes___(___Minutes) No___

Desolation From the Day – <u>Write no more than two sentences</u> on what decreased your faith, your hope and your love for God and neighbor today.

Consolation From the Day – <u>Write no more than two sentences</u> on what increased your faith, your hope and your love for God and neighbor today.

Week 6

Day Two

Spiritual Exercise for Day or Evening

Read this for your Day or Evening Exercise
and reflect on the questions below.

SPIRITUAL RADAR SIGNALS

*HOW GOD SUPPORTS YOU WHEN SIGNALS FROM THE DARKNESS
HAVE TRICKED YOU TO TURN FROM THE LIGHT*

You have studied Ignatius' first two principles for how we ought to act when tempted by the counter inspirations of desolation and here are the last two:

3) God provides the essential support and grace necessary to withstand these times of trial and purification.

The support you need will come from your natural abilities, assisted by Divine grace. You may feel completely overwhelmed by temptations, or the darkness of spirit associated with disordered attractions and compulsive behaviors.

Yet there is sufficient grace for salvation, even if the *logic* of the counter inspiration indicates otherwise! Jesus, the Divine Physician, is *very close to you* during these times of purification. When you encounter the full force and darkness of counter inspirations, be assured that God is present to you <u>even though you may not feel God's presence.</u> Through trial and error, St. Ignatius learned that God is *not* absent.

When you do not feel the Spirit, consciously *thank God, who in complete faithfulness,* will embrace you.

Thank God *aloud* and affirm God's salvific role in your *life.*

4) *Intentionally strive to cultivate patience and persevere in the religious practices of your faith when influenced by the desolation of counter-inspiration.*

The Divine inspiration of consolation always returns but in the interim, we must use the divine means of prayer, penance, and self-examination to resist and gain the most from these times of trial. In this way, we can embrace desolation as an opportunity to deepen our maturing life with God. Be not afraid.

Reflection Exercise:

Pray to the Divine-Inspirer to have your memory "energized." Remember!

What is the one experience or event that makes you question God's love for you? Say it aloud. Now hear the Lord say: "Nothing in the past or the future; no angel or demon; no height or depth; nothing in all of creation will ever separate you from my love in Christ Jesus." (Rom 8:38-39).

Write your experience and God's response in your journal.

Example: *For me, the most powerful modern poem that captures this faithfulness of God is the Footprints Poem. You know it: It has the same wisdom Ignatius uses about trusting God during difficult times. God never leaves us!*

FOOTPRINTS IN THE SAND

One night I dreamed I was walking along
the beach with the Lord. Many scenes
from my life flashed across the sky.

In each scene I noticed footprints in the
sand. Sometimes there were two sets of
footprints, other times there was one
only.

This bothered me because I noticed that
during the low periods of my life, when I
was suffering from anguish, sorrow or
defeat, I could see only one set of
footprints, so I said to the Lord,

"You promised me Lord,
that if I followed you, you would walk
with me always. But I have noticed that
during the most trying periods of my life
there has only been one set of footprints
in the sand. Why, when I needed you
most, have you not been there for me?"

The Lord replied, "The years when you
have seen only one set of footprints, my
child, is when I carried you."

Mary Stevenson, 1936

EXERCISE RECORD

1. When I Awake in the Morning—1 Minute Minimum - 2 Maximum

Location_____ I Exercised Yes___(___Minutes) No___

2. Morning Time Exercise—10 Minutes Minimum -20 Minutes Maximum

Location_____ I Exercised Yes___(___Minutes) No___

3. Examen Exercise Time—15 Minutes Maximum

Location_____ I Exercised Yes___(___Minutes) No___

4. Day Time Exercise—60 Contiguous Minutes (30 or 45 if 60 is not possible)

Location_____ I Exercised Yes___(___Minutes) No___

5. Evening Time Exercise—30 Contiguous Minutes Minimum – 60 Maximum

Location_____ I Exercised Yes___(___Minutes) No___

6. Exercise Journal—1-2 Minutes Once Daily

Location_____ I Exercised Yes___(___Minutes) No___

7. As I Lay Down to Sleep—1 Minute Total

Location_____ I Exercised Yes___(___Minutes) No___

Desolation From the Day – Write no more than two sentences on what decreased your faith, your hope and your love for God and neighbor today.

Consolation From the Day – Write no more than two sentences on what increased your faith, your hope and your love for God and neighbor today.

WEEK 6

DAY THREE

Spiritual Exercise for Day or Evening

I will go to Daily Mass today Alone or with a friend during my Day or Evening Exercise Time. Today I will offer the Mass for peace in the world.

EXERCISE RECORD

1. When I Awake in the Morning—1 Minute Minimum - 2 Maximum

Location_____ I Exercised Yes___(___Minutes) No___

2. Morning Time Exercise—10 Minutes Minimum -20 Minutes Maximum

Location_____ I Exercised Yes___(___Minutes) No___

3. Examen Exercise Time—15 Minutes Maximum

Location_____ I Exercised Yes___(___Minutes) No___

4. Day Time Exercise—60 Contiguous Minutes (30 or 45 if 60 is not possible)

Location_____ I Exercised Yes___(___Minutes) No___

5. Evening Time Exercise—30 Contiguous Minutes Minimum – 60 Maximum

Location_____ I Exercised Yes___(___Minutes) No___

6. Exercise Journal—1-2 Minutes Once Daily

Location_____ I Exercised Yes___(___Minutes) No___

7. As I Lay Down to Sleep—1 Minute Total

Location_____ I Exercised Yes___(___Minutes) No___

Desolation From the Day – Write no more than two sentences on what decreased your faith, your hope and your love for God and neighbor today.

Consolation From the Day – Write no more than two sentences on what increased your faith, your hope and your love for God and neighbor today.

WEEK 6

DAY FOUR

Spiritual Exercise for Day or Evening

Read this for your Day or Evening Exercise
and reflect on the questions below

SPIRITUAL RADAR SIGNALS

*THE FIRST CONDITION THAT OPENS A HEART
TO BECOME PREY TO SIGNALS FROM THE DARKNESS*

At times, God allows us to experience desolation so that we can orient our hearts toward genuine love and our true human nature. In this method, God is showing us the path home by our feeling and experiencing discomfort. Here is the first of three ways we feel this kind of God-given discomfort:

1) *Desolation is directly related to wrong choices in thoughts, words, and deeds made under the influence of the false logic of the counter-inspirations.*

If you stop physical exercise, your body suffers. If you stop your spiritual exercise, your spirit suffers. God removes the divine inspiration of consolation *as a holy warning* that you are straying from your authentic human nature—your heart.

God acts this way to stir your conscience: to remind you to return to authenticity. God allows the loss of consolation so you can *feel* the consequences of your thoughts, words, and deeds associated with counter-inspirational choices. Such false choices will, in due course, erode relationships, creation, human life, faith, hope and love.

Reflection Question:

Pray to the Divine-Inspirer to have your memory "energized." Remember false choices that eroded the very things that God provided for your fulfillment, communion, peace in this life, and eternal joy in the next. Remember!

Remember a time when you were "living true to your heart" and then made a choice to turn from that path in a small or big way. What was the situation and how did you stray? What were the consequences of straying? Remember what it felt like. Did it resemble what we describe as spiritual desolation? Did it perhaps also force you to learn things that have been valuable for you?

Briefly write the context of this choice in your journal and describe how it affected you.

Example: I can remember a time as a priest when I stopped praying the fifteen-minute prayer of the Examen: the very prayer you have been practicing with on this spiritual journey. I was at a point when I felt that advancing my career was more important than taking time to pray and keep in touch with God.

The counter-inspirer deceived me, creating in me the illusion that "my" work was more important that God working in me. Quickly, I became consumed by life's worries and troubles and it took me little time get back on track once I was awakened to the problem.

I now know if a priest can confuse his own skills and talents as more important than his spiritual life, then it can happen to anyone!

EXERCISE RECORD

1. When I Awake in the Morning—1 Minute Minimum - 2 Maximum

Location_____ I Exercised Yes___(___Minutes) No___

2. Morning Time Exercise—10 Minutes Minimum -20 Minutes Maximum

Location_____ I Exercised Yes___(___Minutes) No___

3. Examen Exercise Time—15 Minutes Maximum

Location_____ I Exercised Yes___(___Minutes) No___

4. Day Time Exercise—60 Contiguous Minutes (30 or 45 if 60 is not possible)

Location_____ I Exercised Yes___(___Minutes) No___

5. Evening Time Exercise—30 Contiguous Minutes Minimum – 60 Maximum

Location_____ I Exercised Yes___(___Minutes) No___

6. Exercise Journal—1-2 Minutes Once Daily

Location_____ I Exercised Yes___(___Minutes) No___

7. As I Lay Down to Sleep—1 Minute Total

Location_____ I Exercised Yes___(___Minutes) No___

Desolation From the Day – Write no more than two sentences on what decreased your faith, your hope and your love for God and neighbor today.

Consolation From the Day – Write no more than two sentences on what increased your faith, your hope and your love for God and neighbor today.

WEEK 6

DAY FIVE

Spiritual Exercise for Day or Evening

I will go for a thirty minute walk or run or find a quiet place to sit where I can see nature. I will not listen to music or bring my cell phone with me. I will listen instead to my daydreams, nature and the people who pass by. I will notice people who appear happy and those who seem to be struggling. I will listen to and watch the world God made for my enjoyment, appreciation and engagement. I realize that I have spiritual energy that reaches to the end of the cosmos and beyond. I will attune my radar to what is holy and reject what is evil. I will listen to what brings me joy or makes me sad.

At the end of your walk, run or quiet time speak to God from your heart and ask God to help you with the one thing you need most today in developing your spiritual radar.

EXERCISE RECORD

1. When I Awake in the Morning—1 Minute Minimum - 2 Maximum

Location_____ I Exercised Yes___(___Minutes) No___

2. Morning Time Exercise—10 Minutes Minimum -20 Minutes Maximum

Location_____ I Exercised Yes___(___Minutes) No___

3. Examen Exercise Time—15 Minutes Maximum

Location_____ I Exercised Yes___(___Minutes) No___

4. Day Time Exercise—60 Contiguous Minutes (30 or 45 if 60 is not possible)

Location_____ I Exercised Yes___(___Minutes) No___

5. Evening Time Exercise—30 Contiguous Minutes Minimum – 60 Maximum

Location_____ I Exercised Yes___(___Minutes) No___

6. Exercise Journal—1-2 Minutes Once Daily

Location_____ I Exercised Yes___(___Minutes) No___

7. As I Lay Down to Sleep—1 Minute Total

Location_____ I Exercised Yes___(___Minutes) No___

Desolation From the Day – Write no more than two sentences on what decreased your faith, your hope and your love for God and neighbor today.

Consolation From the Day – Write no more than two sentences on what increased your faith, your hope and your love for God and neighbor today.

WEEK 6

DAY SIX

Spiritual Exercise for Day or Evening

Read this for your Day or Evening Exercise
and reflect on the questions below

SPIRITUAL RADAR SIGNALS

*THE SECOND CONDITION THAT OPENS A HEART
TO BE PREY TO SIGNALS FROM THE DARKNESS*

Here is a second divinely inspired reason we may feel the discomfort of spiritual desolation:

2)   *God allows desolation that is directly linked to your human growth and spiritual progress. God awakens your heart--your spirit, mind and body—to experience its spiritual, emotional and psychological wounds.*

Destructive desires and habits may have taken root in your spirit, mind and body. Spiritual progress and forward movement for a person made in the Divine image is only possible when you awaken and confront this damaging pattern. Sometimes, desolation forces that confrontation. Surviving desolation, we build courage. The Divine Physician helps us identify and uproot desolate appetites and habits by doing spiritual surgery on us—cutting away the bad. Spiritual renewal and healing can, at times, be painful and intense, but through it we awaken to the good.

Ignatius understood this, learning it in life as you yourself are perhaps learning it now. He came to understand that God supports us most especially during the times when we can *feel* lost, condemned by the darkness in our heart, mind and body. He warned: even when you have feelings of desolation, do not be fooled into believing that God does not love and cherish you. Think of the pain any athlete, artist, or musician who must endure a great deal in order to become a leader in their discipline. Leaders are aware of the pain but keep their hearts on the prize.

Reflection Question:

Pray to the Divine-Inspirer to have your memory "energized." Pray to feel deep in your heart that God loves and supports your most authentic self as you suffer the stripping away of the pain, sin, narcissism and wounds that hide your true heart.

Remember one instance in your life in which you felt dread or darkness associated with your false self.

What is the experience you still think about the most, one of false self or narcissism, one that causes you the most pain, still?

Remember it clearly then ask Jesus, "Do you love me through my shame?"

Hear his answer.

Ask for his blessing by telling him you need his help to become a true to your heart's deepest desires.

Hear him respond.

Briefly write about this experience in your journal.

EXERCISE RECORD

1. When I Awake in the Morning—1 Minute Minimum - 2 Maximum

Location_____ I Exercised Yes___(___Minutes) No___

2. Morning Time Exercise—10 Minutes Minimum -20 Minutes Maximum

Location_____ I Exercised Yes___(___Minutes) No___

3. Examen Exercise Time—15 Minutes Maximum

Location_____ I Exercised Yes___(___Minutes) No___

4. Day Time Exercise—60 Contiguous Minutes (30 or 45 if 60 is not possible)

Location_____ I Exercised Yes___(___Minutes) No___

5. Evening Time Exercise—30 Contiguous Minutes Minimum – 60 Maximum

Location_____ I Exercised Yes___(___Minutes) No___

6. Exercise Journal—1-2 Minutes Once Daily

Location_____ I Exercised Yes___(___Minutes) No___

7. As I Lay Down to Sleep—1 Minute Total

Location_____ I Exercised Yes___(___Minutes) No___

Desolation From the Day – Write no more than two sentences on what decreased your faith, your hope and your love for God and neighbor today.

Consolation From the Day – Write no more than two sentences on what increased your faith, your hope and your love for God and neighbor today.

Week 6

Day Seven

Spiritual Exercise for Day or Evening

With one on your faithful friends, do something that you feel fits the spiritual journey you are on.

Perhaps you both want to go to church and pray in silence before God.

You could go to the edge of a stream, a lake, a river, or a park and share time there as you listen, two good friends, to the sounds of God in nature.

Whatever you both need today let it speak to you and lead you and as you enjoy this time together. Write a short reflection on what inspired you in your journal tonight.

EXERCISE RECORD

1. When I Awake in the Morning—1 Minute Minimum - 2 Maximum

Location_____ I Exercised Yes____(____Minutes) No____

2. Morning Time Exercise—10 Minutes Minimum -20 Minutes Maximum

Location_____ I Exercised Yes____(____Minutes) No____

3. Examen Exercise Time—15 Minutes Maximum

Location_____ I Exercised Yes____(____Minutes) No____

4. Day Time Exercise—60 Contiguous Minutes (30 or 45 if 60 is not possible)

Location_____ I Exercised Yes____(____Minutes) No____

5. Evening Time Exercise—30 Contiguous Minutes Minimum – 60 Maximum

Location_____ I Exercised Yes____(____Minutes) No____

6. Exercise Journal—1-2 Minutes Once Daily

Location_____ I Exercised Yes____(____Minutes) No____

7. As I Lay Down to Sleep—1 Minute Total

Location_____ I Exercised Yes____(____Minutes) No____

8. Night Vigils—30 minutes minimum – 45 maximum

Location_____ I Exercised Yes____(____Minutes) No____

Desolation From the Day – Write no more than two sentences on what decreased your faith, your hope and your love for God and neighbor today.

Consolation From the Day – Write no more than two sentences on what increased your faith, your hope and your love for God and neighbor today.

NOTES

NOTES

NIGHT VIGIL

WEEK 6

<u>*THE PHARISEE AND THE PUBLICAN*</u>

The Pharisee and the Tax Collector

Artist Unknown

Spend thirty to forty-five minutes on this Exercise. Do only one section at a time and do not read ahead. Do not feel compelled to finish the whole vigil quickly. Stay with each section until your heart suggests moving on. Do not read or write after this meditation except perhaps a short journal entry. **Be Alone.**

I. Gather in what your senses are experiencing. Breathe in the Spirit of

God. Breathe out whatever is troubling, distracting, or burdensome. Be aware of all the thoughts and feelings coming from the day so far.

II. Talk to Jesus in your own words about your desire for this particular grace: that I may come to know that a true heart—a true leader—is always humble and never proud in a narcissistic way. Pray to Jesus in very personal words that he gives you the knowledge you are loved, even in your sinfulness and weakness. Pray for the grace to know that Jesus our TRUE LEADER learned obedience by suffering on the path of humility. Stay with this for as long as you like. Don't feel compelled to move on unless your heart suggests.

III. Open your Bible and pray with Luke chapter eighteen, verses nine to fourteen. Jesus is instructing his disciples whom he wants to be authentic leaders. He must show them that a true leader is always humble and never proud. Visualize the disciples listening to Jesus and the imaginary scene in the temple describes. Does Jesus make the story serious or humorous? How is he trying to get his disciples to see what real leadership is about in how he describes the story. See and experience the events as they happen. Notice everything about what is happening to Jesus and yourself. Do not move to the next section unless your heart suggests.

IV. ASK THE LORD FOR HELP. Imagine that you are with the disciples as Jesus relates the story of the Pharisee and the publican. Imagine that Jesus turns to you in the crowd and repeats the very last line of the story: "Everyone who exalts himself will be humbled, but the man who humbles himself will be exalted."

How does Jesus say this to you? Does he challenge you or is he praising you? What do you feel as you hear Jesus speak this truth to you? Stop, listen and understand. When you are done, turn to Jesus and say: "Please, Lord, give me a humble heart."

V. Following the meditation, bring your own prayer period to a close by slowly praying the *Our Father,* listening to the words in your heart as you pray.

WEEK 7

DAY ONE

Spiritual Exercise for Day or Evening

Read this for your Day or Evening Exercise
and reflect on the questions below

SPIRITUAL RADAR SIGNALS

*THE THIRD CONDITION THAT OPENS A HEART
TO BECOME TEMPTED BY SIGNALS FROM THE DARKNESS*

Here is the third reason we fall prey to counter-inspiration and spiritual desolation:

3)   *Counter inspirations of desolation may appear during times of spiritual advancement.*

After a period of purification marked by desolation, your heart may find peace in the Divine inspiration of consolation. During these graced rests, you may be tempted to believe the illusion that you have arrived at the end of your spiritual journey. You experience this state of calm and peace as definitive, and feel that you have achieved sanctity, completion, and holiness: that you have it all wrapped up!

During these times, *almost imperceptibly*, a spirit of pride and self-sufficiency takes hold in your heart. "I've completed my discernment training—I am a specialist now." When this happens (when, not if!) the counter inspirations of desolation return *as a warning*.

This happened to St. Ignatius. He felt that he was among the just, and that his spiritual growth was complete, but having experienced desolation, he realized that he was actually *only beginning* on the road to salvation.

God allows this new form of desolation as a warning to remind you that although you have grown in authenticity and holiness, you are still susceptible to the narcissism and destructive pride that will halt all your progress towards true happiness and a heart true to itself.

Be watchful for the first signs of this kid of narcissism and pride-- they usually manifest

> ## TWO ESSENTIAL LESSONS
>
> Cultivate humility during the consoling times of the Divine inspiration. Use your periods of consolation as a preparation for the times of desolation. Be *aware and awake*, always anticipating the return of desolation.
>
> Plan ahead for when desolation makes its return. During your time of consolation, remember how helpless you felt during your time of desolation. This serves as a reminder that *God is the only one* who stabilizes your heart with the Divine inspiration of consolation.

when you feel so satisfied you start to fall away from your spiritual disciplines and practices of your Faith. You might say to yourself: "I am healed;" or, "I don't need those practices anymore;" or "at least I don't heed them as much as I used to!"

We all deceive ourselves and are deceived into believing such things.

Reflection Questions:

Pray to the Divine-Inspirer to have your memory "energized." Remember a time when you thought you had completed your Exercise and just then fell prey to pride. What was the context? Were you surprised that desolation returned when you may have felt on top of the world? Remember the situation and describe it briefly in your journal.

Example: *I had a sabbatical a number of years ago and part of it involved my making a 30-day retreat. This retreat program called for 5 one-hour prayer periods a day. I felt I was sufficiently holy at this point in my life and decided I would only do 3 of the 5.*

God had other plans for me. I felt so much peace in the 3 one-hour prayer periods and less peace when I avoided the other two prayer times. God pulled me in this way to do 5 by giving me great peace and consolation during the 3 periods.

I finally did the 5 and continued them throughout the rest of the retreat. Through this experience I realized how far I had still to grow and was amazed at how proud I had become and out of touch with my own heart.

EXERCISE RECORD

1. When I Awake in the Morning—1 Minute Minimum - 2 Maximum

Location_____ I Exercised Yes___(___Minutes) No___

2. Morning Time Exercise—10 Minutes Minimum -20 Minutes Maximum

Location_____ I Exercised Yes___(___Minutes) No___

3. Examen Exercise Time—15 Minutes Maximum

Location_____ I Exercised Yes___(___Minutes) No___

4. Day Time Exercise—60 Contiguous Minutes (30 or 45 if 60 is not possible)

Location_____ I Exercised Yes___(___Minutes) No___

5. Evening Time Exercise—30 Contiguous Minutes Minimum – 60 Maximum

Location_____ I Exercised Yes___(___Minutes) No___

6. Exercise Journal—1-2 Minutes Once Daily

Location_____ I Exercised Yes___(___Minutes) No___

7. As I Lay Down to Sleep—1 Minute Total

Location_____ I Exercised Yes___(___Minutes) No___

Desolation From the Day – Write no more than two sentences on what decreased your faith, your hope and your love for God and neighbor today.

Consolation From the Day – Write no more than two sentences on what increased your faith, your hope and your love for God and neighbor today.

WEEK 7

DAY TWO

Spiritual Exercise for Day or Evening

I will go for a thirty minute walk or run or find a quiet place to sit where I can see nature. I will not listen to music or bring my cell phone with me. I will listen instead to my daydreams, nature and the people who pass by. I will notice people who appear happy and those who seem to be struggling. I will listen to and watch the world God made for my enjoyment, appreciation and engagement. I realize that I have spiritual energy that reaches to the end of the cosmos and beyond. I will attune my radar to what is holy and reject what is evil. I will listen to what brings me joy or makes me sad.

At the end of your walk, run or quiet time speak to God from your heart and ask God to help you with the one thing you need most today in developing your spiritual radar.

EXERCISE RECORD

1. When I Awake in the Morning—1 Minute Minimum - 2 Maximum

Location_____   I Exercised Yes___(___Minutes) No___

2. Morning Time Exercise—10 Minutes Minimum -20 Minutes Maximum

Location_____   I Exercised Yes___(___Minutes) No___

3. Examen Exercise Time—15 Minutes Maximum

Location_____   I Exercised Yes___(___Minutes) No___

4. Day Time Exercise—60 Contiguous Minutes (30 or 45 if 60 is not possible)

Location_____   I Exercised Yes___(___Minutes) No___

5. Evening Time Exercise—30 Contiguous Minutes Minimum – 60 Maximum

Location_____   I Exercised Yes___(___Minutes) No___

6. Exercise Journal—1-2 Minutes Once Daily

Location_____   I Exercised Yes___(___Minutes) No___

7. As I Lay Down to Sleep—1 Minute Total

Location_____   I Exercised Yes___(___Minutes) No___

Desolation From the Day – Write no more than two sentences on what decreased your faith, your hope and your love for God and neighbor today.

Consolation From the Day – Write no more than two sentences on what increased your faith, your hope and your love for God and neighbor today.

WEEK 7

DAY THREE

Spiritual Exercise for Day or Evening

I will go to Daily Mass today alone or with a friend during my Day or Evening Exercise Time. Offer you Mass today for the individual or group you consider your greatest enemy and ask God to help you forgive them.

EXERCISE RECORD

1. When I Awake in the Morning—1 Minute Minimum - 2 Maximum

Location_____   I Exercised Yes___(___Minutes) No___

2. Morning Time Exercise—10 Minutes Minimum -20 Minutes Maximum

Location_____   I Exercised Yes___(___Minutes) No___

3. Examen Exercise Time—15 Minutes Maximum

Location_____   I Exercised Yes___(___Minutes) No___

4. Day Time Exercise—60 Contiguous Minutes (30 or 45 if 60 is not possible)

Location_____   I Exercised Yes___(___Minutes) No___

5. Evening Time Exercise—30 Contiguous Minutes Minimum – 60 Maximum

Location_____   I Exercised Yes___(___Minutes) No___

6. Exercise Journal—1-2 Minutes Once Daily

Location_____   I Exercised Yes___(___Minutes) No___

7. As I Lay Down to Sleep—1 Minute Total

Location_____   I Exercised Yes___(___Minutes) No___

Desolation From the Day – Write no more than two sentences on what decreased your faith, your hope and your love for God and neighbor today.

Consolation From the Day – Write no more than two sentences on what increased your faith, your hope and your love for God and neighbor today.

WEEK 7

DAY FOUR

Spiritual Exercise for Day or Evening

*GOING DEEPER INTO THE WAYS THE
COUNTER-INSPIRER DECEIVES YOUR HEART AND
TURNS IT AWAY FROM THE LIGHT*

The three exercises that follow this introduction help you discern three attack strategies used by the enemy of human nature to obstruct our spiritual progress.

All three attacks use elements of our life story as weapons against us: our unconscious fears; our psychological and spiritual vulnerabilities; and our long-standing addictive, compulsive and/or sinful habits. These sinful habits do not make us happy but they are familiar behaviors and the *pain of the familiar* is often preferred to *the fear of the unknown*.

Ignatius learned these three attack strategies from his own experience of being deceived during his conversion process. While you might not yet be at a time in your life where you have encountered any of these tactics, rest assured you'll meet them at some point. Notice again that *fear* is the common basis for all lines of attack.

Reflection Question:

Pray to the Divine-Inspirer to have your memory "energized."

Remember! When have you been deceived in the past? If many instances enter your mind, remember the first one that pops in. As you remember that time in your life, think about what tactic was used to trick you.

Then think of other similar times. Is there a pattern? Does the Enemy normally use a certain tactic against you? What are the context/situations it happens most?

Spend a brief time writing in your journal about the lesson that has become the most important for you so far.

Example: *I have learned that we inherit patterns of both grace and sin from our families. One of the experiences I had growing up was how I was disciplined. If I did something wrong, I would be ignored—the equivalent of a "time-out" in the corner—but there would be no communication from my folks, sometimes for days. It was how they were raised and all they knew.*

It had a great impact on my heart. I discovered a very negative way it played out in my adult life. Anytime I would be expecting a response to a request, or a new job, or anything and I did not hear back, I "assumed" I had done something wrong. I would start to feel terrible about myself and get very desolate and depressed.

Gradually, as I grew and deepened my spirituality, I realized that nearly 99% of the time, people had not received my note, or were busy or something completely unrelated to me had delayed their response. It took a long time to "see" this pattern and how it was playing out over and over again.

These are wounds the enemy of human nature uses to make us doubt ourselves and God's love for us.

Watch for similar patterns of grace and sin from your family of origin.

EXERCISE RECORD

1. When I Awake in the Morning—1 Minute Minimum - 2 Maximum

Location_____ I Exercised Yes___(___Minutes) No___

2. Morning Time Exercise—10 Minutes Minimum -20 Minutes Maximum

Location_____ I Exercised Yes___(___Minutes) No___

3. Examen Exercise Time—15 Minutes Maximum

Location_____ I Exercised Yes___(___Minutes) No___

4. Day Time Exercise—60 Contiguous Minutes (30 or 45 if 60 is not possible)

Location_____ I Exercised Yes___(___Minutes) No___

5. Evening Time Exercise—30 Contiguous Minutes Minimum – 60 Maximum

Location_____ I Exercised Yes___(___Minutes) No___

6. Exercise Journal—1-2 Minutes Once Daily

Location_____ I Exercised Yes___(___Minutes) No___

7. As I Lay Down to Sleep—1 Minute Total

Location_____ I Exercised Yes___(___Minutes) No___

Desolation From the Day – Write no more than two sentences on what decreased your faith, your hope and your love for God and neighbor today.

Consolation From the Day – Write no more than two sentences on what increased your faith, your hope and your love for God and neighbor today.

WEEK 7

DAY FIVE

Spiritual Exercise for Day or Evening

I will go for a thirty minute walk or run or find a quiet place to sit where I can see nature. I will not listen to music or bring my cell phone with me. I will listen instead to my daydreams, nature and the people who pass by. I will notice people who appear happy and those who seem to be struggling. I will listen to and watch the world God made for my enjoyment, appreciation and engagement. I realize that I have spiritual energy that reaches to the end of the cosmos and beyond. I will attune my radar to what is holy and reject what is evil. I will listen to what brings me joy or makes me sad.

At the end of your walk, run or quiet time speak to God from your heart and ask God to help you with the one thing you need most today in understanding patterns of sin and grace from my own family.

EXERCISE RECORD

1. When I Awake in the Morning—1 Minute Minimum - 2 Maximum

Location_____   I Exercised Yes___(___Minutes) No___

2. Morning Time Exercise—10 Minutes Minimum -20 Minutes Maximum

Location_____   I Exercised Yes___(___Minutes) No___

3. Examen Exercise Time—15 Minutes Maximum

Location_____   I Exercised Yes___(___Minutes) No___

4. Day Time Exercise—60 Contiguous Minutes (30 or 45 if 60 is not possible)

Location_____   I Exercised Yes___(___Minutes) No___

5. Evening Time Exercise—30 Contiguous Minutes Minimum – 60 Maximum

Location_____   I Exercised Yes___(___Minutes) No___

6. Exercise Journal—1-2 Minutes Once Daily

Location_____   I Exercised Yes___(___Minutes) No___

7. As I Lay Down to Sleep—1 Minute Total

Location_____   I Exercised Yes___(___Minutes) No___

Desolation From the Day – Write no more than two sentences on what decreased your faith, your hope and your love for God and neighbor today.

Consolation From the Day – Write no more than two sentences on what increased your faith, your hope and your love for God and neighbor today.

Week 7

Day Six

Spiritual Exercise for Day or Evening

THE FIRST ATTACK STRATEGY OF THE COUNTER-INSPIRER

FEAR AND PANIC ATTACKS

When you engage your faith practice daily, the enemy of human nature can employ three subtle and malicious lines of attack to discourage you. He will use the weaknesses and fears associated with your vices, your sinful appetites, your compulsive behaviors, your spiritual/psychological wounds, and your broken heart.

This week we will consider the first of the three strategies:

1) *Fear and panic attacks are strategically employed to block growth.*

If you stay committed to the process of uprooting vices, sins, addictions and destructive habits from your life, you will often be attacked with waves of fear and panic. These may try to turn your attention away from your spiritual progress.

Reflection Question:

Pray to the Divine-Inspirer to have your memory "energized." Remember! Think on the times when you were paralyzed by fear or panic attacks. What were the "hooks" that triggered the terrible fear?

For example: was the "hook" your own perfectionism? Did you decide to commit your life more fully to Christ and then had anxiety, panic and dread that you would fail in your attempts to be a better person? Did you start imagining everything that could go wrong, and before you knew it you felt paralyzed?

Remember an example like this in your experience and then look at it carefully—discern what "triggered" the panic? Did you, for instance, hear someone say something relatively harmless that you "heard" as a scary possibility? "You'll do great, kid, just remember not to make a mistake." This comment was innocuous but before you knew it your brain was seeing all the bad possibilities that could play out?

Find your own memories of this kind of paralysis. Sit with the memories for a while. Let yourself understand the deep truth of the attack strategy. It happens to keep you off balance and away from your heart of peace. Pray to "see" the wound or previous fears that initiated this pattern in your life.

Briefly write your memory and what you've learning in your journal.

EXERCISE RECORD

1. When I Awake in the Morning—1 Minute Minimum - 2 Maximum

Location_____ I Exercised Yes____(____Minutes) No____

2. Morning Time Exercise—10 Minutes Minimum -20 Minutes Maximum

Location_____ I Exercised Yes____(____Minutes) No____

3. Examen Exercise Time—15 Minutes Maximum

Location_____ I Exercised Yes____(____Minutes) No____

4. Day Time Exercise—60 Contiguous Minutes (30 or 45 if 60 is not possible)

Location_____ I Exercised Yes____(____Minutes) No____

5. Evening Time Exercise—30 Contiguous Minutes Minimum – 60 Maximum

Location_____ I Exercised Yes____(____Minutes) No____

6. Exercise Journal—1-2 Minutes Once Daily

Location_____ I Exercised Yes____(____Minutes) No____

7. As I Lay Down to Sleep—1 Minute Total

Location_____ I Exercised Yes____(____Minutes) No____

Desolation From the Day – Write no more than two sentences on what decreased your faith, your hope and your love for God and neighbor today.

Consolation From the Day – Write no more than two sentences on what increased your faith, your hope and your love for God and neighbor today.

WEEK 7

DAY SEVEN

Spiritual Exercise for Day or Evening

I will go to Sunday Mass today Alone or with a friend for your Day or Evening Exercise Time. I will offer my Mass today for the issue in my life for which I feel the greatest gratitude and the issue for which I need the most help. I will ask God to bless my family and friends with the same graces.

EXERCISE RECORD

1. When I Awake in the Morning—1 Minute Minimum - 2 Maximum

Location_____ I Exercised Yes___(___Minutes) No___

2. Morning Time Exercise—10 Minutes Minimum -20 Minutes Maximum

Location_____ I Exercised Yes___(___Minutes) No___

3. Examen Exercise Time—15 Minutes Maximum

Location_____ I Exercised Yes___(___Minutes) No___

4. Day Time Exercise—60 Contiguous Minutes (30 or 45 if 60 is not possible)

Location_____ I Exercised Yes___(___Minutes) No___

5. Evening Time Exercise—30 Contiguous Minutes Minimum – 60 Maximum

Location_____ I Exercised Yes___(___Minutes) No___

6. Exercise Journal—1-2 Minutes Once Daily

Location_____ I Exercised Yes___(___Minutes) No___

7. As I Lay Down to Sleep—1 Minute Total

Location_____ I Exercised Yes___(___Minutes) No___

8. Night Vigils—30 minutes minimum – 45 maximum

Location_____ I Exercised Yes___(___Minutes) No___

Desolation From the Day – Write no more than two sentences on what decreased your faith, your hope and your love for God and neighbor today.

Consolation From the Day – Write no more than two sentences on what increased your faith, your hope and your love for God and neighbor today.

NOTES

NOTES

Night Vigil

Week 7

JESUS WALKS ON THE WATER

Walk by Faith by Rebecca Brogran jbtarts.com

Spend thirty to forty-five minutes on this Exercise. Do only one section at a time and do not read ahead. Do not feel compelled to finish each piece of this. Stay with each section until your heart suggests moving on. Do not read or write after this meditation except perhaps a short journal entry. **Be Alone.**

I. Gather in what your senses are experiencing. Breathe in the Spirit of God. Breathe out whatever is troubling, distracting, or burdensome. Be aware of all the thoughts and feelings coming from the day so far.

II. Talk to Jesus in your own words about your desire for this particular grace: that you may learn to overcome dread, fear and panic and follow him in faith no matter the storms that rage.

III. Open your Bible and pray with Matthew chapter fourteen, verses twenty-two through thirty-three. Jesus is instructing his disciples that he is the Lord of all Creation and everything is under his command. He is showing his disciples that they must learn to walk in faith by keeping their true hearts fixed on him and him alone.

Visualize the disciples terrified of Jesus as he walks towards their boat during a raging storm. See the darkness and feel the storm and boat at the point of sinking. See and feel the great fear in the disciples. See also the great love that Peter had for Jesus that leads him to ask Jesus to let him be with him.

Notice: Peter is scared but perseveres but there is still more to learn. When he takes his eyes off of Jesus, he begins to succumb to fear and starts to sink. Notice Jesus rescue him and rebuke him for this lack of faith. Watch and Pray.

IV. ASK THE LORD FOR HIS HELP. Now see yourself with the disciples in the boat. Ask Jesus to let you come to him across the water—to walk by faith. Tell him your fears of walking by faith and ask for the specific help you need to step out of the boat. Mention to him your fears and the patterns you've been remembering in this week's lessons. What does Jesus say to you? What invitation does he extend to you? What help does he give? As you close, say with the other disciples on the boat: "Jesus, you truly are the Son of God!"

V. Following the meditation, bring your own prayer period to a close by slowly praying the *Our Father,* listening to the words in your heart as you pray.

Week 8

Day One

Spiritual Exercise for Day or Evening

Meet with a Spiritual Friend Today

This meeting does not have to be overscheduled. It's important you and your friend do and say those things that will help you to grow in faith.

Theme: Somewhere in your meeting, share questions you have about confronting your fear, dread, and panic attacks. Ask your friend how she or he has been able to deal effectively with fear and panic. Ask your friend to share advice from their own walk of faith in the Lord. As you talk and share, speak aloud to her your greatest hope as you become a person of courage.

One way to get this conversation going is to ask your friend: "What is *your* greatest hope in being a courageous person?" They can share with you what they are learning just as you share your needs, insights, and questions with them.

As you both feel moved, perhaps you can close your time together praying to the Father in the words that Jesus taught us.

EXERCISE RECORD

1. When I Awake in the Morning—1 Minute Minimum - 2 Maximum

Location_____ I Exercised Yes____(____Minutes) No____

2. Morning Time Exercise—10 Minutes Minimum -20 Minutes Maximum

Location_____ I Exercised Yes____(____Minutes) No____

3. Examen Exercise Time—15 Minutes Maximum

Location_____ I Exercised Yes____(____Minutes) No____

4. Day Time Exercise—60 Contiguous Minutes (30 or 45 if 60 is not possible)

Location_____ I Exercised Yes____(____Minutes) No____

5. Evening Time Exercise—30 Contiguous Minutes Minimum – 60 Maximum

Location_____ I Exercised Yes____(____Minutes) No____

6. Exercise Journal—1-2 Minutes Once Daily

Location_____ I Exercised Yes____(____Minutes) No____

7. As I Lay Down to Sleep—1 Minute Total

Location_____ I Exercised Yes____(____Minutes) No____

Desolation From the Day – Write no more than two sentences on what decreased your faith, your hope and your love for God and neighbor today.

Consolation From the Day – Write no more than two sentences on what increased your faith, your hope and your love for God and neighbor today.

WEEK 8

DAY TWO

Spiritual Exercise for Day or Evening

I will go to Daily Mass alone or with a friend for my Day or Evening Exercise Time.

I will pray for myself and my friends and family that we can always overcome our dread, fear and panic of being followers of Jesus. I will pray for myself and my friends and family that we can serve the Lord with free hearts.

EXERCISE RECORD

1. When I Awake in the Morning—1 Minute Minimum - 2 Maximum

Location_____   I Exercised Yes___(___Minutes) No___

2. Morning Time Exercise—10 Minutes Minimum -20 Minutes Maximum

Location_____   I Exercised Yes___(___Minutes) No___

3. Examen Exercise Time—15 Minutes Maximum

Location_____   I Exercised Yes___(___Minutes) No___

4. Day Time Exercise—60 Contiguous Minutes (30 or 45 if 60 is not possible)

Location_____   I Exercised Yes___(___Minutes) No___

5. Evening Time Exercise—30 Contiguous Minutes Minimum – 60 Maximum

Location_____   I Exercised Yes___(___Minutes) No___

6. Exercise Journal—1-2 Minutes Once Daily

Location_____   I Exercised Yes___(___Minutes) No___

7. As I Lay Down to Sleep—1 Minute Total

Location_____   I Exercised Yes___(___Minutes) No___

Desolation From the Day – Write no more than two sentences on what decreased your faith, your hope and your love for God and neighbor today.

Consolation From the Day – Write no more than two sentences on what increased your faith, your hope and your love for God and neighbor today.

Week 8

Day Three

Spiritual Exercise for Day or Evening

THE SECOND ATTACK STRATEGY OF
THE COUNTER-INSPIRER:

FALSE LOVES DISGUISED AS TRUE LOVES

Consider the second of the three attack strategies used by our Enemy:

2) *Narcissism and false values masquerade as true authentic values.*

The enemy can invade our thinking process to portray narcissism as authentic love and to make us see vices as positive values. "Shopping for things I don't need is fine," we think, "in fact it's great because it's a way I bond with my friends." Or: "I am better at _____ than just about everyone else—I'm the best—I've got it made and that's a good thing!"

Your heart can be easily fooled by false loves. All false loves—of shopping or pride or any other vice--are *lusts* masquerading as *love*. They are mirages for parched and anxious hearts hoping to quench their thirst (gluttony, lust, greed, pride, anger, laziness, envy). Instead of providing lasting peace, these illicit loves and illusions merely intensify longings, self-deception, self-preoccupation, and narcissism, ultimately leading to spiritual and psychological death. Giving into these desires just escalates or the narcissism ultimately sets one up for spiritual failure.

In all this, there is a seemingly infinite variety of deception and seductions. They are limited only by the numerous ways a heart can be broken.

God will not sanction these lusts because they issue from a violated heart and lead to your heart's further violation. Once you act upon a false love or deceptive lust, you will most assuredly violate the hearts of others.

Remember: God is Love: the origin, the end, and the defender of the human heart. While God is infinitely merciful with our struggles, God does not sanction anything that breaks your heart--destroys your own or another person's authentic human nature--or leads to your spiritual death. By not sanctioning false loves in you, God is actually doing you a great favor—protecting you! He does this by not enabling you—and hoping that you will one day, very soon, see through the deceptions and return fully to his Heart.

Reflection Exercise:

Pray to the Divine-Inspirer to have your memory "energized." Remember! Name your sins, addictions, and bad habits truthfully as false lovers. In the light of grace, let one or more of them be revealed as neither true servants of the heart nor pathways to the Divine. Expose them! Focus on the main "false love" you need to see *most clearly right now*. Identify it and do the exercise below. When you are done, write a brief journal entry about what you learned today in this Exercise.

Declare to Christ the specific sin, addiction, or destructive compulsion and name it as a false lover.

Describe to Christ the specific sin, addiction or destructive compulsion as coming from the enemy of your human nature.

Descend with Christ into your memory to see and feel your first experience of this specific sin, addiction or compulsion. Ask Christ to compassionately reveal the stress fractures, loneliness and wounds in your heart it promised to satisfy.

Denounce with Christ as your witness, the sin, addiction or destructive compulsion for the ruinous effect in your life, others' lives and society.

Decide with Christ that you will let him heal this wound, diffuse the stress, anxiety and fear feeding it, and transform its damaging effects on your life into the grace of a true heart.

EXERCISE RECORD

1. When I Awake in the Morning—1 Minute Minimum - 2 Maximum

Location_____ I Exercised Yes____(____Minutes) No____

2. Morning Time Exercise—10 Minutes Minimum -20 Minutes Maximum

Location_____ I Exercised Yes____(____Minutes) No____

3. Examen Exercise Time—15 Minutes Maximum

Location_____ I Exercised Yes____(____Minutes) No____

4. Day Time Exercise—60 Contiguous Minutes (30 or 45 if 60 is not possible)

Location_____ I Exercised Yes____(____Minutes) No____

5. Evening Time Exercise—30 Contiguous Minutes Minimum – 60 Maximum

Location_____ I Exercised Yes____(____Minutes) No____

6. Exercise Journal—1-2 Minutes Once Daily

Location_____ I Exercised Yes____(____Minutes) No____

7. As I Lay Down to Sleep—1 Minute Total

Location_____ I Exercised Yes____(____Minutes) No____

Desolation From the Day – Write no more than two sentences on what decreased your faith, your hope and your love for God and neighbor today.

Consolation From the Day – Write no more than two sentences on what increased your faith, your hope and your love for God and neighbor today.

WEEK 8

DAY FOUR

Spiritual Exercise for Day or Evening

I will go for a thirty minute walk or run or find a quiet place to sit where I can see nature. I will not listen to music or bring my cell phone with me. I will listen instead to my daydreams, nature and the people who pass by. I will notice people who appear happy and those who seem to be struggling. I will listen to and watch the world God made for my enjoyment, appreciation and engagement. I realize that I have spiritual energy that reaches to the end of the cosmos and beyond. I will attune my radar to what is holy and reject what is evil. I will listen to what brings me joy or makes me sad.

At the end of your walk, run or quiet time speak to God from your heart and ask God to help you with the one thing you need most today in developing your spiritual radar for false loves in my life.

EXERCISE RECORD

1. When I Awake in the Morning—1 Minute Minimum - 2 Maximum

Location_____   I Exercised Yes____(____Minutes) No____

2. Morning Time Exercise—10 Minutes Minimum -20 Minutes Maximum

Location_____   I Exercised Yes____(____Minutes) No____

3. Examen Exercise Time—15 Minutes Maximum

Location_____   I Exercised Yes____(____Minutes) No____

4. Day Time Exercise—60 Contiguous Minutes (30 or 45 if 60 is not possible)

Location_____   I Exercised Yes____(____Minutes) No____

5. Evening Time Exercise—30 Contiguous Minutes Minimum – 60 Maximum

Location_____   I Exercised Yes____(____Minutes) No____

6. Exercise Journal—1-2 Minutes Once Daily

Location_____   I Exercised Yes____(____Minutes) No____

7. As I Lay Down to Sleep—1 Minute Total

Location_____   I Exercised Yes____(____Minutes) No____

Desolation From the Day – Write no more than two sentences on what decreased your faith, your hope and your love for God and neighbor today.

Consolation From the Day – Write no more than two sentences on what increased your faith, your hope and your love for God and neighbor today.

WEEK 8

DAY FIVE

Spiritual Exercise for Day or Evening

Take time today to speak with one of your closest friends about the journey you are making. Ask them if they have seen any changes in you since you began the journey. Express to them the difficulties and joys of your journey. Give them the freedom to ask you any questions about your journey.

Write in your journal afterwards what you considered the most important elements from the conversation.

What gave you hope, and deepened your faith and love?

If something happened that diminished your faith and love, notice and write that down, too.

EXERCISE RECORD

1. When I Awake in the Morning—1 Minute Minimum - 2 Maximum

Location_____ I Exercised Yes____(___Minutes) No____

2. Morning Time Exercise—10 Minutes Minimum -20 Minutes Maximum

Location_____ I Exercised Yes____(___Minutes) No____

3. Examen Exercise Time—15 Minutes Maximum

Location_____ I Exercised Yes____(___Minutes) No____

4. Day Time Exercise—60 Contiguous Minutes (30 or 45 if 60 is not possible)

Location_____ I Exercised Yes____(___Minutes) No____

5. Evening Time Exercise—30 Contiguous Minutes Minimum – 60 Maximum

Location_____ I Exercised Yes____(___Minutes) No____

6. Exercise Journal—1-2 Minutes Once Daily

Location_____ I Exercised Yes____(___Minutes) No____

7. As I Lay Down to Sleep—1 Minute Total

Location_____ I Exercised Yes____(___Minutes) No____

Desolation From the Day – <u>Write no more than two sentences</u> on what decreased your faith, your hope and your love for God and neighbor today.

Consolation From the Day – <u>Write no more than two sentences</u> on what increased your faith, your hope and your love for God and neighbor today.

WEEK 8

DAY SIX

Spiritual Exercise for Day or Evening

THE THIRD ATTACK STRATEGY OF THE COUNTER-INSPIRER

USE A HARDENED HEART TO DEFEND A BROKEN HEART

This week we examine the third attack strategy used by the Enemy to obstruct our spiritual progress. Just as in the first two lines of attack, *fear* is the main weapon used against you.

3) *When you commit to uprooting sin, addictions, and vices from your body and soul, you will be assaulted by attacks directed at the spiritual and psychological wounds that make you most vulnerable.*

The enemy of human nature can viciously attack you where past pain and wounds have left you most vulnerable. A wall, built with emotional and intellectual counter-inspirations, is erected around the injuries, darkening your conscience. The enemy's purpose in hardening your heart is to keep your emotional and intellectual defenses firmly in place; to keep your conscience dark and your true human nature *hidden*.

Perhaps you felt very hurt after a failed relationship or after your best friend moved away. In response to the pain you became more hardened in your judgments about the meaning of life, truth and beauty. Many normal things in life soon looked grim to you. You gradually stopped trusting people who love you. You started overreacting to people's ordinary, even loving intentions.

The enemy of human nature's chief goal is to *permanently camouflage* your heart. He loves it when you are wounded—this allows him to build walls in you. Jesus made reference to these forms of defensive structures. He said they keep people from believing in Him, even if He should rise from the dead (Lk 16:31), and they grieved Jesus because they harden hearts (Mk 3: 5).

Reflection Exercise:

Pray to the Divine-Inspirer to have your memory "energized." Remember! Think of one hard-hearted position you have taken that goes against the Gospel's and the Church's teachings of love. Remember all the intellectual arguments you make, internally or with others, that "justify" a position you know in your heart to be too extreme.

Bring your thoughts to Jesus in this exercise. See him sitting with you. Tell him what you believe and why you think yourself justified in holding it. What does Jesus, who is the truth and the model of human nature, say? What does he invite you to understand? Does he challenge you in anyway? What do you say in return?

Write your experiences briefly in your journal.

Example: *A person shared on a retreat how he had lost his virginity in high school. He was deeply in love with the girl and the event took place in his family home. He felt afterwards that he betrayed his parent's trust (they were away). And the very next day, the girl dumped him. She had simply "used" him for her own pleasure.*

Since this was his first sexual relationship, his self-confidence suffered terribly. His heart was hardened twice—once over the shame of having betrayed his parent's trust and once over being "used." Both his relationship with his parents and women suffered. He shut his parents out of his life and started to "use" girls the way he had been used. But he felt justified because of the "hardness of his heart."

He only later realized how his heart had been broken by his own shame and by the pain of being used. It took many years to see how he was treating his parents and women and finally had the grace to change—to after being allowed to "see" what had happened.

EXERCISE RECORD

1. When I Awake in the Morning—1 Minute Minimum - 2 Maximum

Location_____ I Exercised Yes___(___Minutes) No___

2. Morning Time Exercise—10 Minutes Minimum -20 Minutes Maximum

Location_____ I Exercised Yes___(___Minutes) No___

3. Examen Exercise Time—15 Minutes Maximum

Location_____ I Exercised Yes___(___Minutes) No___

4. Day Time Exercise—60 Contiguous Minutes (30 or 45 if 60 is not possible)

Location_____ I Exercised Yes___(___Minutes) No___

5. Evening Time Exercise—30 Contiguous Minutes Minimum – 60 Maximum

Location_____ I Exercised Yes___(___Minutes) No___

6. Exercise Journal—1-2 Minutes Once Daily

Location_____ I Exercised Yes___(___Minutes) No___

7. As I Lay Down to Sleep—1 Minute Total

Location_____ I Exercised Yes___(___Minutes) No___

Desolation From the Day – Write no more than two sentences on what decreased your faith, your hope and your love for God and neighbor today.

Consolation From the Day – Write no more than two sentences on what increased your faith, your hope and your love for God and neighbor today.

WEEK 8

DAY SEVEN

Spiritual Exercise for Day or Evening

I will go to Sunday Mass today alone or with a friend for my Day or Evening Exercise Time. I will offer my Mass today for myself, my family and friends that where we might be hardened due to a broken heart, God will bring light and healing.

EXERCISE RECORD

1. When I Awake in the Morning—1 Minute Minimum - 2 Maximum

Location_____ I Exercised Yes___(___Minutes) No___

2. Morning Time Exercise—10 Minutes Minimum -20 Minutes Maximum

Location_____ I Exercised Yes___(___Minutes) No___

3. Examen Exercise Time—15 Minutes Maximum

Location_____ I Exercised Yes___(___Minutes) No___

4. Day Time Exercise—60 Contiguous Minutes (30 or 45 if 60 is not possible)

Location_____ I Exercised Yes___(___Minutes) No___

5. Evening Time Exercise—30 Contiguous Minutes Minimum – 60 Maximum

Location_____ I Exercised Yes___(___Minutes) No___

6. Exercise Journal—1-2 Minutes Once Daily

Location_____ I Exercised Yes___(___Minutes) No___

7. As I Lay Down to Sleep—1 Minute Total

Location_____ I Exercised Yes___(___Minutes) No___

8. Night Vigils—30 minutes minimum – 45 maximum

Location_____ I Exercised Yes___(___Minutes) No___

Desolation From the Day – Write no more than two sentences on what decreased your faith, your hope and your love for God and neighbor today.

Consolation From the Day – Write no more than two sentences on what increased your faith, your hope and your love for God and neighbor today.

NOTES

NOTES

NIGHT VIGIL

WEEK 8

THE BEHEADING OF ST. JOHN THE BAPTIST

The Beheading of St. John the Baptist by Pierre Puvis de Chavannes

Spend thirty to forty-five minutes on this Exercise. Do only one section at a time and do not read ahead. Do not feel compelled to finish the whole exercise. Stay with each section until your heart suggests moving on. Do not read or write after this meditation except perhaps a short journal entry. **Be Alone.**

I. Gather in what your senses are experiencing. Breathe in the Spirit of God. Breathe out whatever is troubling, distracting, or burdensome. Be aware of all the thoughts and feelings coming from the day so far.

II. Talk to Jesus in your own words about your desire for this particular grace: that I may learn to love him so much that I would, if the time came, offer my very life for him and his leadership in the world. Pray for the grace to be more in love with Christ and his light, than to fear those who follow the enemy in darkness. Pray for the grace to give your life's blood for Christ the King. Stay with this for as long as you like. Don't feel compelled to move on unless your heart suggests.

III. Open your Bible and pray with Matthew chapter fourteen, verses one through twelve. As you read, be aware of this: John the Baptist was the greatest prophet in Israel's history. He is the pivot point between the old and new Covenants. He, like you, was known by Christ in his mother's womb. From the moment Mary visited Elizabeth and the child John leapt, he was blessed by Christ to be the herald of the Lamb of God coming into the world. Like Jesus said, "of those born of women, none is greater than John."

Now see John imprisoned for challenging Herod's marriage. See the party as it unfolds and the hatred and jealously of Herodias' mother. See this courageous prophet in the fullness of his manhood through the pledge of a coward who succumbs to the hatred of his wife. Be at the party. Watch events as they unfold. See, smell, sense all that is happening. Feel Jesus' Spirit from afar sensing what is happening to his herald and champion.

What is in Jesus heart as he feels John's life ended? Watch and pray. See and experience the events as they happen. Notice everything about what is happening to Jesus and yourself. Do not move to the next section unless your heart suggests.

IV. ASK THE LORD FOR HIS HELP. You are with Jesus as the news is brought to him of John's murder. Hear Jesus say to you: "The least in the Kingdom is greater than John. Do you still want to be my follower knowing the price? What do you say to Jesus? What then, does he say to you in return? Listen.

V. Following the meditation, bring your own prayer period to a close by slowly praying the *Our Father,* listening to the words in your heart as you pray.

WEEK 9

DAY ONE

I will go for a thirty minute walk or run or find a quiet place to sit where I can see nature. I will not listen to music or bring my cell phone with me. I will listen instead to my daydreams, nature and the people who pass by. I will notice people who appear happy and those who seem to be struggling. I will listen to and watch the world God made for my enjoyment, appreciation and engagement. I realize that I have spiritual energy that reaches to the end of the cosmos and beyond. I will attune my radar to what is holy and reject what is evil. I will listen to what brings me joy or makes me sad.

At the end of your walk, run or quiet time speak to God from your heart and ask God to help you with the one thing you need most today in developing your spiritual radar.

EXERCISE RECORD

1. When I Awake in the Morning—1 Minute Minimum - 2 Maximum

Location_____   I Exercised Yes___(___Minutes) No___

2. Morning Time Exercise—10 Minutes Minimum -20 Minutes Maximum

Location_____   I Exercised Yes___(___Minutes) No___

3. Examen Exercise Time—15 Minutes Maximum

Location_____   I Exercised Yes___(___Minutes) No___

4. Day Time Exercise—60 Contiguous Minutes (30 or 45 if 60 is not possible)

Location_____   I Exercised Yes___(___Minutes) No___

5. Evening Time Exercise—30 Contiguous Minutes Minimum – 60 Maximum

Location_____   I Exercised Yes___(___Minutes) No___

6. Exercise Journal—1-2 Minutes Once Daily

Location_____   I Exercised Yes___(___Minutes) No___

7. As I Lay Down to Sleep—1 Minute Total

Location_____   I Exercised Yes___(___Minutes) No___

Desolation From the Day – Write no more than two sentences on what decreased your faith, your hope and your love for God and neighbor today.

Consolation From the Day – Write no more than two sentences on what increased your faith, your hope and your love for God and neighbor today.

WEEK 9

DAY TWO

Spiritual Exercise for Day or Evening

A COUNTER-INSPIRER STORY

A HEARDENED HEART COVERING A BROKEN HEART

In our daily social media, we can observe evidence of hardened hearts camouflaging broken hearts. On a news blog, a teenager won a court case, forcing a public high school to remove a banner in the school's gym that referred to "Our Heavenly Father." The student was a baptized Roman Catholic who stopped believing in God at ten years of age when her mother fell ill.

"I had always been told that if you pray, God will always be there when you need Him," the student said. "And it didn't happen for me, and I doubted it had happened for anybody else. So yeah, I think that was just like the last step, and after that I just really didn't believe any of it."

Much of the media framed the story as a legal and constitutional fight to prevent state-sponsored religion. But another plot-line can be detected in this story. The student opposed religious expression because of deep childhood wounds. The student's mother fell ill and

"God did not listen" to a prayer for healing. At the bottom of this story is a deeply wounded heart.

We must remember: the enemy will do anything to keep a person distracted from the interior wound. So distracted, the person does not heal. The "fight" the enemy "inspires" will appear noble to some, including the broken hearted, but through the lens of *discernment*, we can see that the person is blind to the pride, intellectual justifications, and defiance that conceal the understandable fear and pain of a ten-year old child's broken heart over her mother's death.

So it is with many people and the "noble causes" they fight for. Many causes are noble but many are also the outgrowth of wounded and terrified people running away from their pain. In fact, much of the violence perpetrated between persons, groups, and countries in our own day is generated by wounded hearts seeking revenge for their suffering.

> DISCERNMENT WISDOM
>
> Here is an old Rwandan proverb:
>
> *"You can outdistance that which is running after you, but not what is running inside of you."*
>
> In other words, you need to find out the things in your heart that are upsetting you and making you think, speak and act in ways that are contrary to your true heart so they can be minimized.

As you become attuned to the spiritual world, look at the world with new eyes. Watch or read news of conflicts waged everywhere. Violence, be it economic, intellectual, physical, psychological, or verbal, can be self-justified and is often hidden behind nationalism, false religion, jihadism, extreme laws or cultural norms and mob mentality. Notice how many of the perpetrators of these conflicts are wounded, hardened, and unable to show mercy.

Reflection Exercise:

Pray to the Divine-Inspirer to have your memory "energized." Remember! Have you ever been a crusader for a cause whose "energy" to pursue the cause was from a hidden hurt or anger? If so, remember how the enemy of human nature instigated your intellectual arguments, fostered your sense of injustice, and promoted defiance against legitimate authority.

Ask the Lord, "What motivated *my* crusade at that point in my life? Where did I hurt?" Listen for answers. Then ask, "Help me to heal, and forgive me in the same way that I seek to forgive others. Help me spend the energy of my life to produce fruit that endures to eternity."

Write briefly in your journal about your memories and any thoughts that come to you.

EXERCISE RECORD

1. When I Awake in the Morning—1 Minute Minimum - 2 Maximum

Location_____ I Exercised Yes___(___Minutes) No___

2. Morning Time Exercise—10 Minutes Minimum -20 Minutes Maximum

Location_____ I Exercised Yes___(___Minutes) No___

3. Examen Exercise Time—15 Minutes Maximum

Location_____ I Exercised Yes___(___Minutes) No___

4. Day Time Exercise—60 Contiguous Minutes (30 or 45 if 60 is not possible)

Location_____ I Exercised Yes___(___Minutes) No___

5. Evening Time Exercise—30 Contiguous Minutes Minimum – 60 Maximum

Location_____ I Exercised Yes___(___Minutes) No___

6. Exercise Journal—1-2 Minutes Once Daily

Location_____ I Exercised Yes___(___Minutes) No___

7. As I Lay Down to Sleep—1 Minute Total

Location_____ I Exercised Yes___(___Minutes) No___

Desolation From the Day – Write no more than two sentences on what decreased your faith, your hope and your love for God and neighbor today.

Consolation From the Day – Write no more than two sentences on what increased your faith, your hope and your love for God and neighbor today.

WEEK 9

DAY THREE

Spiritual Exercise for Day or Evening

I will go to Daily Mass alone or with a friend for my Day or Evening Exercise Time.

I will pray for myself and my companions that we will always have God's grace in us to make the sacrifices we need to make, including the giving up of our wounds, sins, and fears, so that we may grow in spiritual freedom!

EXERCISE RECORD

1. When I Awake in the Morning—1 Minute Minimum - 2 Maximum

Location_____ I Exercised Yes___(___Minutes) No___

2. Morning Time Exercise—10 Minutes Minimum -20 Minutes Maximum

Location_____ I Exercised Yes___(___Minutes) No___

3. Examen Exercise Time—15 Minutes Maximum

Location_____ I Exercised Yes___(___Minutes) No___

4. Day Time Exercise—60 Contiguous Minutes (30 or 45 if 60 is not possible)

Location_____ I Exercised Yes___(___Minutes) No___

5. Evening Time Exercise—30 Contiguous Minutes Minimum – 60 Maximum

Location_____ I Exercised Yes___(___Minutes) No___

6. Exercise Journal—1-2 Minutes Once Daily

Location_____ I Exercised Yes___(___Minutes) No___

7. As I Lay Down to Sleep—1 Minute Total

Location_____ I Exercised Yes___(___Minutes) No___

Desolation From the Day – <u>Write no more than two sentences</u> on what decreased your faith, your hope and your love for God and neighbor today.

Consolation From the Day – <u>Write no more than two sentences</u> on what increased your faith, your hope and your love for God and neighbor today.

WEEK 9

DAY FOUR

Spiritual Exercise for Day or Evening

SUPER-ADVANCED SPIRITUAL RADAR STRATEGIES TO DISTINGUISH
THE DIVINE-INSPIRER FROM THE COUNTER-INSPIRER:

<u>*STRATEGIES ONE THROUGH THREE*</u>

It can be difficult to differentiate between Divine inspirations and counter-inspirations, especially because a counter-inspiration can *appear* as a genuine good, or *feel* authentic. Ignatius understood this and provided eight strategies for discerning the difference between the Divine-Inspirer's and the counter-inspirer's tactics at a more advanced and nuanced level of spiritual development. Today we will consider the first three of eight discernments.

First Discernment: The Divine-Inspirer works to give you true joy and happiness. This is accomplished by eliminating all sadness and upset caused by the enemy of your human nature. The counter-inspirer on the other hand works against such joy and happiness. He does this most successfully by using false reasoning, subtleties, and layers of deceptions.

You will know the presence of the enemy because the enemy's

arguments will be logical, yet leave you feeling anxious, discouraged, hopeless and possibly cynical. The Divine-Inspirer's arguments will fill your soul with hope.

Second Discernment: The Divine-Inspirer alone can work *directly* on your heart and soul. The Divine-Inspirer can touch your soul at will—the enemy can seem to do so but is really only creating the illusion of touching your soul. What does the Divine-Inspirer promote by his spiritual visits?

✠ Increased love of God and love of innocence

✠ Humility, selflessness, and surrender of the control of your life to God

✠ A listening spirit capable of accepting and affirming the Commandments, the teachings of Christ, and divinely revealed and definitively proclaimed matters of belief held by the Church to be true.

Third Discernment: Both the Divine-Inspirer and the counter-inspirer can *inspire* your will, but with *opposite goals*. The Divine-Inspirer seeks to promote genuine human freedom, authenticity, and spiritual/psychological growth in harmony with your authentic human nature. The counter-inspirer seeks to erode genuine human freedom and to disintegrate your spiritual and psychological health. The enemy's goal is to damage your authentic human nature and move you further from your true heart.

Reflection Exercise:

Pray to the Divine-Inspirer to have your memory "energized."

Remember back to a time when your happiness was undermined by "inspirations" that seemed "good" or "logical" but left you feeling anxious, discouraged or hopeless.

Remember another time when the Divine-Inspirer built up your faith, hope and love through his very real and true inspirations. This will be a time when you were inspired and moved toward faith, hope and love— toward your authentic self.

Be brave, too, and remember a time you were "inspired" away from your freedom and had your heart and peace undermined, even disintegrated for a while—what did you do to regain it?

Be brief, ask to be inspired, and write in your journal whatever you remember.

EXERCISE RECORD

1. When I Awake in the Morning—1 Minute Minimum - 2 Maximum

Location_____ I Exercised Yes____(___Minutes) No____

2. Morning Time Exercise—10 Minutes Minimum -20 Minutes Maximum

Location_____ I Exercised Yes____(___Minutes) No____

3. Examen Exercise Time—15 Minutes Maximum

Location_____ I Exercised Yes____(___Minutes) No____

4. Day Time Exercise—60 Contiguous Minutes (30 or 45 if 60 is not possible)

Location_____ I Exercised Yes____(___Minutes) No____

5. Evening Time Exercise—30 Contiguous Minutes Minimum – 60 Maximum

Location_____ I Exercised Yes____(___Minutes) No____

6. Exercise Journal—1-2 Minutes Once Daily

Location_____ I Exercised Yes____(___Minutes) No____

7. As I Lay Down to Sleep—1 Minute Total

Location_____ I Exercised Yes____(___Minutes) No____

Desolation From the Day – <u>Write no more than two sentences</u> on what decreased your faith, your hope and your love for God and neighbor today.

Consolation From the Day – <u>Write no more than two sentences</u> on what increased your faith, your hope and your love for God and neighbor today.

WEEK 9

DAY FIVE

Spiritual Exercise for Day or Evening

I will go for a thirty minute walk or run or find a quiet place to sit where I can see nature. I will not listen to music or bring my cell phone with me. I will listen instead to my daydreams, nature and the people I pass by. I will notice people who appear happy and those who seem to be struggling. I will listen to and watch the world God made for my enjoyment, appreciation and engagement. I realize that I have spiritual energy that reaches to the end of the cosmos and beyond. I will attune my radar to what is holy and reject what is evil. I will listen to what brings me joy or makes me sad.

At the end of your walk, run or quiet time speak to God from your heart and ask for guidance with the one thing that would help you most as you develop your spiritual radar for these more nuanced and subtle tactics of discernment.

EXERCISE RECORD

1. When I Awake in the Morning—1 Minute Minimum - 2 Maximum

Location_____ I Exercised Yes____(____Minutes) No____

2. Morning Time Exercise—10 Minutes Minimum -20 Minutes Maximum

Location_____ I Exercised Yes____(____Minutes) No____

3. Examen Exercise Time—15 Minutes Maximum

Location_____ I Exercised Yes____(____Minutes) No____

4. Day Time Exercise—60 Contiguous Minutes (30 or 45 if 60 is not possible)

Location_____ I Exercised Yes____(____Minutes) No____

5. Evening Time Exercise—30 Contiguous Minutes Minimum – 60 Maximum

Location_____ I Exercised Yes____(____Minutes) No____

6. Exercise Journal—1-2 Minutes Once Daily

Location_____ I Exercised Yes____(____Minutes) No____

7. As I Lay Down to Sleep—1 Minute Total

Location_____ I Exercised Yes____(____Minutes) No____

Desolation From the Day – Write no more than two sentences on what decreased your faith, your hope and your love for God and neighbor today.

Consolation From the Day – Write no more than two sentences on what increased your faith, your hope and your love for God and neighbor today.

WEEK 9

DAY SIX

Spiritual Exercise for Day or Evening

SUPER-ADVANCED SPIRITUAL
RADAR STRATEGIES TO DISTINGUISH
THE DIVINE-INSPIRER FROM THE COUNTER-INSPIRER:

STRATEGIES FOUR AND FIVE

Today we consider the fourth and fifth of eight strategies for discerning the difference between the Divine-Inspirer's and the counter-inspirer's tactics.

Fourth Discernment: The Divine-Inspirer asks us to always remember that the counter-inspirer can mimic the Divine-Inspirer in thoughts, feelings, and desires. The counter-inspirer's purpose in doing so is to lead you in the wrong direction: similar to Ignatius' experience with his damaging habit of re-confessing old sins. The counter-inspirer wants to lead you away from your true heart.

Fifth Discernment: Distinguishing the difference between Divine and counter inspirations requires you to develop the habit of examining the *overall trajectory* of your thoughts and desires. If the beginning, middle, and end are directed to what is genuine and right, the inspirations are from the Divine-Inspirer. If, however, the trajectory of the desires and thoughts lead to:

✠ something contrary to the Commandments or the precepts of Christ's Church;

✠ or they distract and weaken your aspirations for selflessness;

✠ or they in some way diminish the good plans and goals you had previously established;

then they are a product of the counter-inspirer.

Ignatius was distracted by his re-confession habit—he kept confessing his sins over and over again without finding peace. His aspirations for following the path of conversion were undermined by this tendency. When he realized this, he identified the influence of the counter-inspirer, and surrendered the damaging habit. This choice began the process of dismantling his narcissistic pride *at its root*.

Ignatius once remarked that human beings are no match for the subtle temptations of the enemy of human nature, but God is! God is indeed a match for the enemy's temptations. *Never dialogue with the enemy of your human nature.* Speak only to Christ, and let Christ deal with the enemy of your human nature. Trust your life, your heart and your soul to Christ.

Reflection Exercise:

Pray to the Divine-Inspirer to have your memory "energized." Remember! Write briefly in your journal about one instance in your life where strategies four and five appeared to be influencing you. Think of a time you were "inspired" to do something but it led you away from Christ and the Commandments, made you more self-centered, moved you from your previous positive goals and desires.

What was the situation? Can you trace the "inspiration" back to how you thought it would work out more positively? How did you end up "seeing through" the illusion of the false inspiration? Remember this and celebrate your strength in Christ.

Example: *I was a freshman in high school when I started smoking cigarettes. By the time I entered the Jesuits in the 1970s, I was smoking two packs a day. I remember I felt "inspired" to give them up before I started my 30-day retreat as a sacrifice to open my life more to God.*

A wise novice master, hearing my rationale, would not let me quit right then. He said you can quit after the retreat. He "discerned" that my "inspiration" was not from God but was designed to distract me from the graces of the retreat.

He was dead accurate! When I finally did quit smoking after the retreat, I was inspired to begin an intense exercise regimen at the same time to get back in shape. I started the regimen and it was so difficult to not smoke <u>and</u> do my exercise regimen that I nearly gave up both disciplines!

Here again, the enemy of human nature "inspired" me to take on too much in the hopes I would fail at both. I decided to get through the quitting phase of smoking and later I would exercise. Without the power of discernment in me, I would not have understood how to do what was best and right for my spiritual and human development.

EXERCISE RECORD

1. When I Awake in the Morning—1 Minute Minimum - 2 Maximum

Location_____ I Exercised Yes___(___Minutes) No___

2. Morning Time Exercise—10 Minutes Minimum -20 Minutes Maximum

Location_____ I Exercised Yes___(___Minutes) No___

3. Examen Exercise Time—15 Minutes Maximum

Location_____ I Exercised Yes___(___Minutes) No___

4. Day Time Exercise—60 Contiguous Minutes (30 or 45 if 60 is not possible)

Location_____ I Exercised Yes___(___Minutes) No___

5. Evening Time Exercise—30 Contiguous Minutes Minimum – 60 Maximum

Location_____ I Exercised Yes___(___Minutes) No___

6. Exercise Journal—1-2 Minutes Once Daily

Location_____ I Exercised Yes___(___Minutes) No___

7. As I Lay Down to Sleep—1 Minute Total

Location_____ I Exercised Yes___(___Minutes) No___

Desolation From the Day – Write no more than two sentences on what decreased your faith, your hope and your love for God and neighbor today.

Consolation From the Day – Write no more than two sentences on what increased your faith, your hope and your love for God and neighbor today.

Week 9

Day Seven

Spiritual Exercise for Day or Evening

I will go to Sunday Mass today alone or with a friend for my Day or Evening Exercise Time. Today I will offer my Mass for the national or international situation that appears to me most in need of healing.

EXERCISE RECORD

1. When I Awake in the Morning—1 Minute Minimum - 2 Maximum

Location_____   I Exercised Yes____(____Minutes) No____

2. Morning Time Exercise—10 Minutes Minimum -20 Minutes Maximum

Location_____   I Exercised Yes____(____Minutes) No____

3. Examen Exercise Time—15 Minutes Maximum

Location_____   I Exercised Yes____(____Minutes) No____

4. Day Time Exercise—60 Contiguous Minutes (30 or 45 if 60 is not possible)

Location_____   I Exercised Yes____(____Minutes) No____

5. Evening Time Exercise—30 Contiguous Minutes Minimum – 60 Maximum

Location_____   I Exercised Yes____(____Minutes) No____

6. Exercise Journal—1-2 Minutes Once Daily

Location_____   I Exercised Yes____(____Minutes) No____

7. As I Lay Down to Sleep—1 Minute Total

Location_____   I Exercised Yes____(____Minutes) No____

8. Night Vigils—30 minutes minimum – 45 maximum

Location_____   I Exercised   Yes____(____Minutes) No____

Desolation From the Day – Write no more than two sentences on what decreased your faith, your hope and your love for God and neighbor today.

Consolation From the Day – Write no more than two sentences on what increased your faith, your hope and your love for God and neighbor today.

NOTES

NOTES

NIGHT VIGIL

WEEK 9

Joseph's Dream by Mikalojus Ciurlionis

Spend thirty to forty-five minutes on this Exercise. Do only one section at a time and do not read ahead. Do not feel compelled to finish the whole exercise immediately. Stay with each section until your heart suggests moving on. Do not read or write after this meditation except perhaps a short journal entry. ***Be Alone.***

I. Gather in what your senses are experiencing. Breathe in the Spirit of God. Breathe out whatever is troubling, distracting, or burdensome. Be aware of all the thoughts and feelings coming from the day so far.

II. Talk to Jesus in your own words about your desire for this particular grace: that you may always listen to dreams inspired by messengers who visit you both while awake and while asleep. Pray to God, "May I not be afraid to follow what seems impossible. Give me the grace to know that you have planned for me a beautiful life that will set my heart free." Stay with this for as long as you like. Don't feel compelled to move on unless your heart suggests.

III. Open your Bible and pray with Matthew chapter one, verses eighteen through twenty-five. As you read, be aware: Joseph was a good and honorable man. He followed the most gentle and compassionate course in deciding to divorce Mary quietly. He indeed loved God with his whole heart, mind and soul and his neighbor as himself. How heartbroken he was that his plan for marriage with Mary was not possible. His dream for his life was crushed.

God had something even greater in mind for this man. To reach Joseph, God had to inspire him in a dream in which Joseph was given courage to follow his heart even though he had no way of knowing what it all meant or how it would work. "Joseph son of David, do not be afraid" the messenger said to him.

As you read, watch Joseph going to sleep deeply sad. Watch the angel visit him and touch his mind and heart as he sleeps. See him discover a new plan as the messenger speaks to his soul. Watch as he awakes with wonder and awe. Do not move to the next section unless your heart suggests.

IV. ASK THE LORD FOR HIS HELP. You have dreams for your own life that might not seem possible. Tell Jesus what makes them impossible and why you are sad. Ask Jesus to send his Spirit to your spirt to help you not to be afraid of what comes next. Ask Jesus to fulfill your life's dream. What is it? What does Jesus offer to you? Tell him if it frightens you and ask for courage. What does he offer to you? How do you respond to his dream? What do you say to Jesus? What then, does he say to you in return? Listen.

V. Following the meditation, bring your own prayer period to a close by slowly praying the *Our Father,* listening to the words in your heart as you pray.

Week 10

Day One

Spiritual Exercise for Day or Evening

*SUPER-ADVANCED SPIRITUAL RADAR STRATEGIES TO DISTINGUISH THE
DIVINE-INSPIRER FROM THE COUNTER-INSPIRER:*

<u>*STRATEGY SIX*</u>

Today we consider the sixth of eight strategies for discerning the difference between the Divine-Inspirer's and the counter-inspirer's tactics.

Sixth Discernment: As you develop the habit of tracing the trajectory of thoughts and desires that have led you away from God, do not become discouraged. Practice does indeed make perfect. In your life, you will fall for the bait of the counter-inspirer countless times. The main point is to keep trying, keep discerning. Once you stop this discernment process, you can lose yourself terribly, so keep going!

Practically speaking, commit now to a process in which, when you are triggered by the strategy the counter-inspirer uses, you recognize it. Commit to admitting in your heart your personal vulnerabilities, since they are what the enemy of your authentic human nature manipulates. Discernment is a courageous process in which you develop new habits of intentional consciousness.

Example: *Here's an example of how I do this in my life. I was pushed hard to perform in school when I was growing up and became a perfectionist. If I did not get an "A," I felt bad—a failure. A "B" grade was always second best. I carried this attitude to everything I tried to master.*

When I entered the Jesuits at eighteen and started getting spiritual guidance in my life, I could begin to see that I learned I am "good" if I "win." And if I don't win, I am not good. The passion to "win" could be easily manipulated by the enemy so that I didn't try things I wanted to do because I might "fail," or I tended to quit things I needed to do because I could not excel.

Again, "fear" was the motivator behind all of this, and so was pride. I had to grow up and see the hidden pride behind my perfectionism that was basically saying, "I will save myself by my perfect actions."

At this level of conversion, the enemy's tactics work on your concealed pride, vanity, and narcissism—the Original Sin of the human family. When you think or feel: "I do not need God," "I will control my own life," "I will set my own rules", or "I will be my own savior," rest assured, the enemy of human nature is at work!

Reflection Exercise:

Pray to the Divine-Inspirer to have your memory "energized." Remember! Write briefly in your journal about a time when the counter-inspirer hooked into your pride and self-centeredness. Remember how you felt that you didn't need God or were not humble before God. What inspired the pattern or thought? How did this trajectory happen? When did you realize you had been duped by the counter-inspirer? Can you trace the "inspiration" back to how you thought it would work out more positively? Remember, the counter-inspirer will use the same strategy on you as long as it works! Be brief in your writing.

EXERCISE RECORD

1. When I Awake in the Morning—1 Minute Minimum - 2 Maximum

Location_____ I Exercised Yes___(___Minutes) No___

2. Morning Time Exercise—10 Minutes Minimum -20 Minutes Maximum

Location_____ I Exercised Yes___(___Minutes) No___

3. Examen Exercise Time—15 Minutes Maximum

Location_____ I Exercised Yes___(___Minutes) No___

4. Day Time Exercise—60 Contiguous Minutes (30 or 45 if 60 is not possible)

Location_____ I Exercised Yes___(___Minutes) No___

5. Evening Time Exercise—30 Contiguous Minutes Minimum – 60 Maximum

Location_____ I Exercised Yes___(___Minutes) No___

6. Exercise Journal—1-2 Minutes Once Daily

Location_____ I Exercised Yes___(___Minutes) No___

7. As I Lay Down to Sleep—1 Minute Total

Location_____ I Exercised Yes___(___Minutes) No___

Desolation From the Day – Write no more than two sentences on what decreased your faith, your hope and your love for God and neighbor today.

Consolation From the Day – Write no more than two sentences on what increased your faith, your hope and your love for God and neighbor today.

WEEK 10

DAY TWO

Spiritual Exercise for Day or Evening

I will go to Daily Mass alone or with a friend today. I will ask the grace for myself that I can remember the most significant experiences that have most helped me become more true to my heart and God's life in me during this journey.

EXERCISE RECORD

1. When I Awake in the Morning—1 Minute Minimum - 2 Maximum

Location_____   I Exercised Yes___(___Minutes) No____

2. Morning Time Exercise—10 Minutes Minimum -20 Minutes Maximum

Location_____   I Exercised Yes___(___Minutes) No____

3. Examen Exercise Time—15 Minutes Maximum

Location_____   I Exercised Yes___(___Minutes) No____

4. Day Time Exercise—60 Contiguous Minutes (30 or 45 if 60 is not possible)

Location_____   I Exercised Yes___(___Minutes) No____

5. Evening Time Exercise—30 Contiguous Minutes Minimum – 60 Maximum

Location_____   I Exercised Yes___(___Minutes) No____

6. Exercise Journal—1-2 Minutes Once Daily

Location_____   I Exercised Yes___(___Minutes) No____

7. As I Lay Down to Sleep—1 Minute Total

Location_____   I Exercised Yes___(___Minutes) No____

Desolation From the Day – Write no more than two sentences on what decreased your faith, your hope and your love for God and neighbor today.

Consolation From the Day – Write no more than two sentences on what increased your faith, your hope and your love for God and neighbor today.

WEEK 10

DAY THREE

Spiritual Exercise for Day or Evening

*SUPER-ADVANCED SPIRITUAL RADAR STRATEGIES TO DISTINGUISH THE
DIVINE-INSPIRER FROM THE COUNTER-INSPIRER:*

STRATEGY SEVEN

Today we consider the seventh of eight strategies for discerning the
difference between the Divine-Inspirer's and the counter-inspirer's
tactics.

Seventh Discernment: When you are progressing towards authenticity,
innocence, and genuine human freedom, the Divine-Inspirer produces
delight in you. A sense of electrical energy, anxious excitement, or a
restless need to make hasty decisions gives way to a calmer patience
and tranquility.

This is about both the *feelings* (anxious or calm) and the *trajectory*
(towards or away from authenticity). If you are moving *toward* God, the
enemy of your human nature will inspire "black noise," creating anxious
thoughts and urgent feelings. The enemy wants to discourage you from
turning to God. As you move away from God, God will inspire you with
alarm bells that signal, "You are entering dangerous territory!" You have
the choice of what noise or music to listen to. Gradually and with God's
help, you will work to find your way back to joy.

Reflection Exercise:

Pray to the Divine-Inspirer to have your memory "energized." Remember! Write briefly in your journal of a time you felt an anxious energy or "black noise" to stay in a pattern of life that was not in line with your truest self.

How did you get back to your senses? Did a friend tell you to "stop overthinking" and just go with the flow? Did an adult provide insight you needed? Did prayer work to help you?

Be brief and ask to be inspired as you remember and write!

FALLING IN LOVE

Nothing is more practical than finding God--that is,
than falling in love in a quite absolute final way.
What you are in love with,
what seizes your imagination,
will affect everything.
It will decide what will get you out of bed in the morning,
what you do with your evenings,
how you spend your weekend,
what you read, who you know,
what breaks your heart,
and what amazes you with joy and gratitude.
Fall in love,
stay in love,
and it will decide everything.

Pedro Arrupe, S.J.

EXERCISE RECORD

1. When I Awake in the Morning—1 Minute Minimum - 2 Maximum

Location_____ I Exercised Yes___(___Minutes) No___

2. Morning Time Exercise—10 Minutes Minimum -20 Minutes Maximum

Location_____ I Exercised Yes___(___Minutes) No___

3. Examen Exercise Time—15 Minutes Maximum

Location_____ I Exercised Yes___(___Minutes) No___

4. Day Time Exercise—60 Contiguous Minutes (30 or 45 if 60 is not possible)

Location_____ I Exercised Yes___(___Minutes) No___

5. Evening Time Exercise—30 Contiguous Minutes Minimum – 60 Maximum

Location_____ I Exercised Yes___(___Minutes) No___

6. Exercise Journal—1-2 Minutes Once Daily

Location_____ I Exercised Yes___(___Minutes) No___

7. As I Lay Down to Sleep—1 Minute Total

Location_____ I Exercised Yes___(___Minutes) No___

Desolation From the Day – Write no more than two sentences on what decreased your faith, your hope and your love for God and neighbor today.

Consolation From the Day – Write no more than two sentences on what increased your faith, your hope and your love for God and neighbor today.

WEEK 10

DAY FOUR

Spiritual Exercise for Day or Evening

I will go for a thirty minute walk or run or find a quiet place to sit where I can see nature. I will not listen to music or bring my cell phone with me. I will listen instead to my daydreams, nature, and the people I pass by. I will notice people who appear happy and those who seem to be struggling. I will listen to and watch the world God made for my enjoyment, appreciation and engagement. I will listen to what brings me joy or makes me sad. If I feel inspired, I will pray a Rosary while I walk so that my heart becomes more spiritually alert.

At the end of your walk, run or quiet time speak to God from your heart and ask God to help you with the one thing you need most today in developing your spiritual radar especially as regards to "feelings" and spiritual "trajectories."

EXERCISE RECORD

1. When I Awake in the Morning—1 Minute Minimum - 2 Maximum

Location_____ I Exercised Yes____(____Minutes) No____

2. Morning Time Exercise—10 Minutes Minimum -20 Minutes Maximum

Location_____ I Exercised Yes____(____Minutes) No____

3. Examen Exercise Time—15 Minutes Maximum

Location_____ I Exercised Yes____(____Minutes) No____

4. Day Time Exercise—60 Contiguous Minutes (30 or 45 if 60 is not possible)

Location_____ I Exercised Yes____(____Minutes) No____

5. Evening Time Exercise—30 Contiguous Minutes Minimum – 60 Maximum

Location_____ I Exercised Yes____(____Minutes) No____

6. Exercise Journal—1-2 Minutes Once Daily

Location_____ I Exercised Yes____(____Minutes) No____

7. As I Lay Down to Sleep—1 Minute Total

Location_____ I Exercised Yes____(____Minutes) No____

Desolation From the Day – <u>Write no more than two sentences</u> on what decreased your faith, your hope and your love for God and neighbor today.

Consolation From the Day – <u>Write no more than two sentences</u> on what increased your faith, your hope and your love for God and neighbor today.

WEEK 10

DAY FIVE

Spiritual Exercise for Day or Evening

*SUPER-ADVANCED SPIRITUAL RADAR STRATEGIES TO DISTINGUISH
THE DIVINE-INSPIRER FROM THE COUNTER-INSPIRER:*

STRATEGY EIGHT

Today we consider the eighth of eight strategies for discerning the difference between the Divine-Inspirer's and the counter-inspirer's tactics.

Eighth Discernment: You will know an inspiration is from the Divine-Inspirer because it produces an intense sense of devotion and love. You feel a sense of selflessness and willing surrender of your life to God's control. The inspirations help you understand and trust received Tradition, the Commandments, and the precepts of Christ as proclaimed by the Church.

However, you can be led astray in the after-glow of such inspiration and grace. You can be led astray by your own ideas or by the influence of the counter-inspirer. Thus, Ignatius warns us to be highly attentive during the time just after Divine inspirations. Be cautious and make no revisions, commitments, or plans during this time unless your discernments are clear as to the source of the inspiration.

Reflection Exercise:

Pray to the Divine-Inspirer to have your memory "energized." Remember! Write briefly in your journal as best as you can recall one instance in your life where strategy eight came into view. Specifically write about a time when you were living/feeling hopeful and in tune with God and your heart—"on top of the world" and feeling that you would always be clear about what was good and right. Did an "afterglow" trick you to move away from God?

DISCERNMENT - UNIVERSAL TRUTHS AND VALUES

The Ten Commandments revealed to Israel are part of God's plan to bring back into human consciousness the universal truths of "right relationship." All the Commandments are about "relationships."

Ignatius anchors his Rules to the Commandments so that a person can know if the spiritual "inspirations' they receive are authentic or not.

Ignatius' Rules of Discernment are universal because "spiritual discernment" does not change due to cultural norms, religions or history. It is anchored to human nature crafted in the Divine image. This is the whole point of a "universal" value or truth. A heart that is "attuned" will hear what is authentic---Deep calls to Deep Ps. 42: 7

As a heart seeking Christ, you are moving deep into the faith to find a way of living that will set the world on fire! To do that, you are attuning your heart to values and truths that are universal.

Example: *We can remember St. Ignatius' experience of making his life confession. It was a graced experience to make that confession. Yet, he launched himself into an obsessive habit of confession after that initial event that nearly derailed his conversion process.*

So be very careful about "afterglows" and the suggestions they "inspire." Be brief and ask to be inspired as you remember something for your journal!

EXERCISE RECORD

1. When I Awake in the Morning—1 Minute Minimum - 2 Maximum

Location_____ I Exercised Yes___(___Minutes) No___

2. Morning Time Exercise—10 Minutes Minimum -20 Minutes Maximum

Location_____ I Exercised Yes___(___Minutes) No___

3. Examen Exercise Time—15 Minutes Maximum

Location_____ I Exercised Yes___(___Minutes) No___

4. Day Time Exercise—60 Contiguous Minutes (30 or 45 if 60 is not possible)

Location_____ I Exercised Yes___(___Minutes) No___

5. Evening Time Exercise—30 Contiguous Minutes Minimum – 60 Maximum

Location_____ I Exercised Yes___(___Minutes) No___

6. Exercise Journal—1-2 Minutes Once Daily

Location_____ I Exercised Yes___(___Minutes) No___

7. As I Lay Down to Sleep—1 Minute Total

Location_____ I Exercised Yes___(___Minutes) No___

Desolation From the Day – Write no more than two sentences on what decreased your faith, your hope and your love for God and neighbor today.

Consolation From the Day – Write no more than two sentences on what increased your faith, your hope and your love for God and neighbor today.

WEEK 10

DAY SIX

Spiritual Exercise for Day or Evening

I will go for a thirty minute walk or run or find a quiet place to sit where I can see nature. I will not listen to music or bring my cell phone with me. I will listen instead to my daydreams, nature, and the people who pass by. I will notice people who appear happy and those who seem to be struggling. I will listen to and watch the world God made for my enjoyment, appreciation and engagement. I will listen to what brings me joy or makes me sad. If I feel inspired, I will pray a Rosary while I walk so that my heart becomes more spiritually alert.

At the end of your walk, run or quiet time speak to God from your heart and ask God to help you with the one thing you need most today in developing your spiritual radar especially in paying attention to inspirations in the state of an afterglow of consolation.

EXERCISE RECORD

1. When I Awake in the Morning—1 Minute Minimum - 2 Maximum

Location_____   I Exercised Yes___(___Minutes) No___

2. Morning Time Exercise—10 Minutes Minimum -20 Minutes Maximum

Location_____   I Exercised Yes___(___Minutes) No___

3. Examen Exercise Time—15 Minutes Maximum

Location_____   I Exercised Yes___(___Minutes) No___

4. Day Time Exercise—60 Contiguous Minutes (30 or 45 if 60 is not possible)

Location_____   I Exercised Yes___(___Minutes) No___

5. Evening Time Exercise—30 Contiguous Minutes Minimum – 60 Maximum

Location_____   I Exercised Yes___(___Minutes) No___

6. Exercise Journal—1-2 Minutes Once Daily

Location_____   I Exercised Yes___(___Minutes) No___

7. As I Lay Down to Sleep—1 Minute Total

Location_____   I Exercised Yes___(___Minutes) No___

Desolation From the Day – Write no more than two sentences on what decreased your faith, your hope and your love for God and neighbor today.

Consolation From the Day – Write no more than two sentences on what increased your faith, your hope and your love for God and neighbor today.

WEEK 10

DAY SEVEN

Take an Thirty Minutes Today for
This Exercise on Discernment

Reflection Exercise:

Fill in the sentence with what you have learned from your own life.

"Just like St. Ignatius' Divine inspiration to reform his life was corrupted into a damaging habit of confessing old sins, I've realized that my divine inspiration is corrupted by

_____."

"I know now that the counter-inspirer hurts me by manipulating my long-standing vulnerabilities which are:

_____."

"I understand that the Divine-Inspirer will always offer the graces and insights to lead me home. Here's how I've come to understand this:

_____."

Remember the victory that is assured for you in Christ's birth, life, death and resurrection. Ask God to fully activate this sense of assurance in your life.

As you work with God's grace to let your life be transformed into your truest self, never be discouraged by your failings, sins and weaknesses.

The Divine Physician will never tire of forgiving you. Never tire of coming to Him for forgiveness. In this radical, loving trust, you encounter the unfathomable and unbounded mercy of God.

Reflection Exercise:

Pray to the Divine-Inspirer to have your memory "energized." Remember!

Write briefly in your journal as best as you can recall the one major lesson you learned from the previous eight strategies discussed in the last two weeks of the spiritual journey for a heart true to itself.

Write a crucial insight you gained from meeting with your friends.

Pray to be inspired and write briefly in your journal one or two lessons you "never want to forget!" Be brief but specific.

EXERCISE RECORD

1. When I Awake in the Morning—1 Minute Minimum - 2 Maximum

Location_____ I Exercised Yes____(____Minutes) No____

2. Morning Time Exercise—10 Minutes Minimum -20 Minutes Maximum

Location_____ I Exercised Yes____(____Minutes) No____

3. Examen Exercise Time—15 Minutes Maximum

Location_____ I Exercised Yes____(____Minutes) No____

4. Day Time Exercise—60 Contiguous Minutes (30 or 45 if 60 is not possible)

Location_____ I Exercised Yes____(____Minutes) No____

5. Evening Time Exercise—30 Contiguous Minutes Minimum – 60 Maximum

Location_____ I Exercised Yes____(____Minutes) No____

6. Exercise Journal—1-2 Minutes Once Daily

Location_____ I Exercised Yes____(____Minutes) No____

7. As I Lay Down to Sleep—1 Minute Total

Location_____ I Exercised Yes____(____Minutes) No____

8. Night Vigils—30 minutes minimum – 45 maximum

Location_____ I Exercised Yes____(____Minutes) No____

Desolation From the Day – Write no more than two sentences on what decreased your faith, your hope and your love for God and neighbor today.

Consolation From the Day – Write no more than two sentences on what increased your faith, your hope and your love for God and neighbor today.

NOTES

NOTES

NIGHT VIGIL

WEEK 10

THE BAPTISM OF JESUS

*Spend thirty to forty-five minutes on this exercise. Do only one section at a time and do not read ahead. Do not feel compelled to finish the whole vigil in each intricate part. Stay with each section until your heart suggests moving on. Do not read or write after this meditation except perhaps a short journal entry. **Be Alone.***

I. Gather in what your senses are experiencing. Breathe in the Spirit of God. Breathe out whatever is troubling, distracting, or burdensome. Be aware of all the thoughts and feelings coming from the day so far.

The Baptism of Christ by Tintoretto

II. Talk to Jesus in your own words about your desire for this particular grace: that I may always submit to my heart and live in humility so I can be one with Jesus and also his disciple--beloved of the Father. May I not be afraid to follow the vocation/mission I know in my heart for which I have been baptized. May I know in my heart that Jesus wants me as his disciple so he can honor me one day in his Kingdom before the Father. Stay with this for as long as you like. Don't feel compelled to move on unless your heart suggests.

III. Open your Bible and pray with John chapter one, verses twenty-four through thirty-four and Matthew chapter three, verses twenty-one and twenty-two. Watch John and Jesus as the events you read unfold. See the crowd. What is their mood? Are they young and old? Be in the crowd watching this pivotal moment in the life of Jesus. See Jesus in the river and watch him as the water is poured over his head and body and notice the expression on his face and on the face of John who baptizes him. Can you sense what Jesus is thinking and feeling? What John is thinking and feeling? What the assembled crowd is thinking and feeling?

IV. ASK THE LORD FOR HIS HELP. After the descent of the Holy Spirit, notice that Jesus sees you in the crowd and invites you to be with him in the Jordan. He reaches out to take your hand. He tells you are beloved to him and he wants you as his disciple.

Imagine it just like this. See Jesus take the sea shell from John and with water from the Jordan, pour it over your head and body. See how he looks to heaven and tells his Father: "Father (put your name here) is to be with me in my mission. Confirm (put your name here) in the vocation you have placed in his/her Heart."

How do you feel now? What is the exact vocation/mission he has placed on your Heart? Listen to Jesus' words as he defines your vocation with you—*your way* of following him into service for others. Let him take both your hands and speak to you from his heart to yours. As he does, feel your common vocation with Jesus: to bring the Father's light and salvation to the world.

V. Following the meditation, bring your own prayer period to a close by slowly praying the *Our Father,* listening to the words in your heart as you pray.

ENDNOTES

[1] William M. Watson, SJ, *Forty Weeks: An Ignatian Path to Christ* (Seattle: Sacred Story Press, 2013), 196-200.

[2] GOD WILLED HUMAN NATURE [Catechism of the Catholic Church from here forward-"CCC" #362-8].

The human person, created in the image of God, is a being at once corporeal and spiritual. The biblical account expresses this reality in symbolic language when it affirms that "then the LORD God formed man of dust from the ground, and breathed into his nostrils the breath of life; and man became a living being." [*Gen* 2:7.] **Man, whole and entire, is therefore *willed* by God (emphasis supplied).** In Sacred Scripture the term "soul" often refers to human *life* or the entire human *person*. [Cf. *Mt* 16:25-26; *Jn* 15:13; *Acts* 2:41.] But "soul" also refers to the innermost aspect of man, that which is of greatest value in him, [Cf. *Mt* 10:28; 26:38; *Jn* 12:27; *2 Macc* 6:30.] that by which he is most especially in God's image: "soul" signifies the *spiritual principle* in man.

The human body shares in the dignity of "the image of God": it is a human body precisely because it is animated by a spiritual soul, and it is the whole human person that is intended to become, in the body of Christ, a temple of the Spirit: [Cf. *1 Cor* 6:19-20; 15:44-45.]

Man, though made of body and soul, is a unity. Through his very bodily condition he sums up in himself the elements of the material world. Through him they are thus brought to their highest perfection and can raise their voice in praise freely given to the Creator. For this reason man may not despise his bodily life. Rather he is obliged to regard his body as good and to hold it in honor since God has created it and will raise it up on the last day. [GS 14 § 1; cf. Dan 3:57-80.]

The unity of soul and body is so profound that one has to consider the soul to be the "form" of the body: [Cf. Council of Vienne (1312): DS 902.] i.e., it is because of its spiritual soul that the body made of matter becomes a living, human body; spirit and matter, in man, are not two natures united, but rather their union forms a single nature.

The Church teaches that every spiritual soul is created immediately by God - it is not "produced" by the parents - and also that it is immortal: it does not perish when it separates from the body at death, and it will be reunited with the body at the final

Resurrection. [Cf. Pius XII, *Humani Generis*: DS 3896; Paul VI, *CPG* § 8; Lateran Council V (1513): DS 1440.]

Sometimes the soul is distinguished from the spirit: St. Paul for instance prays that God may sanctify his people "wholly", with "spirit and soul and body" kept sound and blameless at the Lord's coming. [*1 Thess* 5:23.] The Church teaches that this distinction does not introduce a duality into the soul. [Cf. Council of Constantinople IV (870): DS 657.] "Spirit" signifies that from creation man is ordered to a supernatural end and that his soul can gratuitously be raised beyond all it deserves to communion with God. [Cf. Vatican Council I, *Dei Filius*: DS 3005; GS 22 § 5; *Humani Generis*: DS 3891.]

The spiritual tradition of the Church also emphasizes the *heart*, in the biblical sense of the depths of one's being, where the person decides for or against God. [Cf. *Jer* 31:33; *Deut* 6:5; 29:3; *Isa* 29:13; *Ezek* 36:26; *Mt* 6:21; *Lk* 8:15; *Rom*.5:5.]

[3] MAN IN PARADISE [CCC #374-9]

The first man was not only created good, but was also established in friendship with his Creator and in harmony with himself and with the creation around him, in a state that would be surpassed only by the glory of the new creation in Christ.

The Church, interpreting the symbolism of biblical language in an authentic way, in the light of the New Testament and Tradition, teaches that our first parents, Adam and Eve, were constituted in an original "state of holiness and justice". [Cf. Council of Trent (1546): DS 1511.] This grace of original holiness was "to share in divine life". [Cf. *LG* 2.]

By the radiance of this grace all dimensions of man's life were confirmed. As long as he remained in the divine intimacy, man would not have to suffer or die. [Cf. *Gen* 2:17; 3:16,19.] The inner harmony of the human person, the harmony between man and woman, [Cf. *Gen* 2:25.] and finally the harmony between the first couple and all creation, comprised the state called "original justice."

The "mastery" over the world that God offered man from the beginning was realized above all within man himself: *mastery of self*. The first man was unimpaired and ordered in his whole being because he was free from the triple concupiscence [Cf. *1 Jn* 2:16.] that subjugates him to the pleasures of the senses, covetousness for earthly goods, and self-assertion, contrary to the dictates of reason.

The sign of man's familiarity with God is that God places him in the garden. [Cf. *Gen* 2:8.] There he lives "to till it and keep it." Work is not yet a burden [*Gen* 2:15; cf. 3:17-19] but rather the collaboration of man and woman with God in perfecting the visible creation. This entire harmony of original justice, foreseen for man in God's plan, will be lost by the sin of our first parents.

[4] A poetic way to describe the creation of human nature, Original Sin and God's work of redemption in Christ comes from a revelation on Divine Providence given to Saint Catherine of Sienna:

"With a look of mercy that revealed his indescribable kindness, God the Father spoke to Catherine: Beloved daughter, everything I give to man comes from the love and care I have for him. I desire to show my mercy to the whole world and my protective love to all those who want it. But in his ignorance man treats himself very cruelly. My care is constant, but he turns my life-giving gifts into a source of death. Yes, I created him with loving care and formed him in my image and likeness. I pondered, and I was moved by the beauty of my creation. I gave him a memory to recall my goodness, for I wanted him to share in my own power. I gave him an intellect to know and understand my will through the wisdom of my Son, for I am the giver of every good gift and I love him with a father's constant love. Through the Holy Spirit I gave him a will to love what he would come to know with his intellect.

In my loving care I did all this, so that he could know me and perceive my goodness and rejoice to see me for ever. But as I have recounted elsewhere, heaven had been closed off because of Adam's disobedience. Immediately after his sin all manner of evil made its advance throughout the world.

So that I might commute the death consequent upon this disobedience, I attended to you with loving care—out of provident concern I handed over my only-begotten Son to make satisfaction for your needs. I demanded supreme obedience from him so that the human race might be freed of the poison which had infected the entire earth because of Adam's disobedience. With eager love he submitted to a shameful death on the cross and by that death he gave you life, not merely human but divine. (Cap. 134, ed. Latina, Ingolstadii 1583, ff² 215v-216).

[5] Dom Bruno Webb, *Why Does God Permit Evil* (Manchester, Sophia Institute Press, 2004), 70.

[6] On July 27, 2016, Pope Francis met with the Polish bishops during his time at World Youth Day. Pope Francis addressed the issue of human nature and persons created in God's image by saying we are living in times that seek to change this reality. In the published transcript of the meeting Francis said: "We are living a moment of the annihilation of man as image of God. And I would like to end here with this aspect,

because behind this are ideologies. In Europe, in America, in Latin America, in Africa, in some countries of Asia, there are ideological colonizations. And one of these – I say it clearly with name and surname "is *gender*! Today children, children are taught this in school that one can choose one's sex! And why do they teach this? Because the books <used> are those of individuals and institutions that give money. They are ideological colonizations, supported also by very influential countries. And this is terrible. Speaking with Pope Benedict, who is well and has clear thinking, he said to me: "Holiness, this is the time of the sin against God the Creator!" He is intelligent! God has created man and woman; God created the world thus, and thus, and thus..., and we are doing the opposite. God has given us an "untilled" state, so that we can till it; and then, with this tilling, we are doing things that are taking us back to the "untilled" state! We must think about what Pope Benedict said: It's the time of the sin against God the Creator!" And this will help us."

[7] Invite God to be with you all day long:

Traditional Morning Offering

O Jesus, through the Immaculate Heart of Mary,
I offer you my prayers, works, joys, and sufferings of this day
for all the intentions of your Sacred Heart,
in union with the Holy Sacrifice of the Mass throughout the world,
for the salvation of souls, the reparation of sins, the reunion of all Christians,
and in particular for the intentions of the Holy Father this month. Amen.

I arise to-day :
might of Heaven
brightness of Sun
whiteness of Snow
splendour of Fire
speed of Light
swiftness of Wind
depth of Sea
stability of Earth
firmness of Rock.

I arise to-day :
Might of God
Power of God
Wisdom of God
Eye of God
Ear of God

Word of God

Hand of God

Path of God

Shield of God

Host of God

(Morning Prayer from The Book of Cerne, 9th C)

St Michael Prayer Before Opening Eyes

[8] Holy Michael, the Archangel, defend us in battle. Be our safeguard against the wickedness and snares of the devil. May God rebuke him, we humbly pray; and do you, O Prince of the heavenly host, by the power of God cast into hell Satan and all the evil spirits who wander through the world seeking the ruin of souls.

Amen.

[9] Go to sacredstory.net and click on the MEMBERS tab on the upper right corner. Sign up to be a member-- it is free. Open the Members page and then open the Forty Weeks Audio and Video Resources. Under Audio Resources, you will see MEDITATION. This is the 15 minute Examen prayer we use for Sacred Story. Download it and use it on your phone or home system for a guided meditation version of the Daily Examen. Described in the Spiritual Exercises for the Daily Journey.

[10] A suggestion: Use this name to address God and/or Jesus every time you naturally think of God throughout the day. For example, you may say in your heart before a meeting: "Lord Jesus, be with me now." Say it, and then just move on with your meeting. Do not make this a tedious exercise, but one that feels natural and relaxed. You do not have to think long and hard about God. The purpose of this spontaneous prayer is just a short, friendly reminder of God's presence. Use this name if you find yourself conversing with God during the day.

sacredstoryrpress.com

Sacred Story Press explores dynamic new dimensions of classic Ignatian spirituality, based on St. Ignatius' Conscience Examen in the *Sacred Story* prayer method pioneered by Fr. Bill Watson, S.J. We are creating a new class of spiritual resources. Our publications are research-based, authentic to the Catholic Tradition and designed to help individuals achieve integrated, spiritual growth and holiness of life.

We Request Your Feedback

The Sacred Story Institute welcomes feedback on *Forty Weeks*. Contact us via email or letter. Give us ideas, suggestions and inspirations for how to make this a better resource for Catholics and Christians of all ages and walks of life.

For bulk orders and group discounts, contact us:
admin-team@sacredstory.net

Sacred Story Institute & Sacred Story Press
1401 E. Jefferson Suite 405
Seattle, Washington, 98122

ABOUT THE AUTHOR

Fr. William Watson, S.J., D. Min., has spent over thirty-five years developing Ignatian programs and retreats He has collaborated extensively with Fr. Robert Spitzer in the last fifteen years on Ignatian retreats for corporate CEO's. In the spring of 2011 he launched a non-profit institute to bring Ignatian Spirituality to Catholics of all ages and walks of life. The Sacred Story Institute is promoting third millennium evangelization for the Society of Jesus and the Church by using the time-tested *Examination of Conscience* of St. Ignatius.

Fr. Watson has served as: Director of Retreat Programs at Georgetown University; Vice President for Mission at Gonzaga University; and Provincial Assistant for International Ministries for the Oregon Province of the Society of Jesus. He holds Masters Degrees in Divinity and Pastoral Studies, respectively (1986; Weston Jesuit School of Theology, Cambridge Massachusetts). He received his Doctor of Ministry degree in 2009 from The Catholic University of America (Washington D.C.).

Made in the USA
Middletown, DE
23 September 2018